The First-Year Experience Monograph Series

Shedding Light on Sophomores:

An Exploration of the Second College Year

Barbara F. Tobolowsky and Bradley E. Cox, *Editors*

National Resource Center for The First-Year Experience® & Students in Transition • University of South Carolina, 2007

Cite as:

Tobolowsky, B. F., & Cox, B. E. (2007). *Shedding light on sophomores: An exploration of the second college year* (Monograph No. 47). Columbia, SC: University of South Carolina, National Resource Center for The First-Year Experience & Students in Transition.

Sample chapter citation:

Schaller, M. A. (2007). The development of college sophomores. In B. F. Tobolowsky & B. E. Cox (Eds.), *Shedding light on sophomores: An exploration of the second college year* (Monograph No. 47, pp. 1-11). Columbia, SC: University of South Carolina, National Resource Center for The First-Year Experience & Students in Transition.

Special thanks to the staff of the National Resource Center who made this project possible:

Angie Mellor, Graphic Artist, for layout and design; Tracy Skipper, Editorial Projects Coordinator, and Asheley Bice, Graduate Assistant, for copyediting; Trish Willingham, Assistant Editor, and Dottie Weigel, Graduate Assistant, for proofing.

Additional copies of this book may be ordered from the National Resource Center for The First-Year Experience and Students in Transition, University of South Carolina, 1728 College Street, Columbia, SC, 29208. Telephone (803) 777-6229. Fax (803) 777-4699.

ISBN 978-1-889271-57-6

Library of Congress Cataloging-in-Publication Data

Shedding light on sophomores : an exploration of the second college year / Barbara F. Tobolowsky and Bradley Cox, editors.

p. cm. -- (The first-year experience monograph series ; no. 47)

Includes bibliographical references and index.

ISBN-13: 978-1-889271-57-6 (alk. paper)

1. College sophomores--United States. 2. College students--United States. I. Tobolowsky, Barbara F. II. Cox, Bradley E.

LA229.S49 2007

378.1'98--dc22

2007027977

Table of Contents

Foreword

The Advancement of Sophomore Initiatives

Jerry Pattengale & Laurie Schreiner

When we produced the first sophomore monograph in 2000 (Schreiner & Pattengale), we were able to identify around 40 colleges with initiatives dedicated to sophomore issues; only a few of these had fully developed programs. Seven years later, as this current monograph reveals, nearly 130 institutions responded to the National Survey of Sophomore-Year Initiatives, sharing information regarding programs they designed specifically for second-year students. This increase suggests that a wave of sophomore programming is hitting four-year colleges, reminiscent of the beginning of first-year efforts that now are commonplace nationally. Today, institutional strategic plans, curricular offerings, and conference presentations represent a growing recognition of second-year issues and their impact on student success and persistence to graduation.

While we are pleased to see this increase in attention to the second year, we are even more pleased that significant progress has been made toward the 10 recommendations that concluded our 2000 monograph (Gardner, Pattengale, & Schreiner). As we read this current monograph, it was clear to us that there have been noteworthy developments in several key areas that can inform the decisions and programming surrounding the sophomore year.

The key recommendation from our earlier monograph suggested that attention be given to the advising area, since there was substantial evidence pointing to sophomores' need for meaning and purpose as they made decisions about a major and a career. There appears to be considerable progress in this area, as 61% of colleges participating in the national survey reported advising programs specifically designed to meet sophomores' needs. The most common sophomore initiative involved advising that was focused on major selection and career planning. This finding was good news to us, but it also raises an issue concerning resources and time. Advising in the sophomore year is by necessity focused more on personal goals, helping students find a sense of direction for their lives, and providing assistance with the career planning process. These are time-consuming activities that go far beyond course registration; as a result, many institutions need to redirect faculty and staff resources to address the unique needs of their sophomores. Some excellent examples of how campuses have accomplished this reallocation are provided throughout this monograph and represent models that can be replicated by other institutions facing the same challenges.

A second area where strong recommendations were made in the 2000 monograph related to collecting data about sophomore transitions, both nationally and locally. Very little research had been conducted on the sophomore experience at that time, and too often decisions about campus programming were made without gathering the information needed from the students themselves. As can be seen throughout this monograph, significant strides have been made in researching the sophomore experience, particularly from a qualitative perspective in order to hear their voices. As a result, an increasing number of campuses report data-driven practices, and national studies such as the Indiana Project on Academic Success (funded by the Lumina Foundation) are taking shape.

A third area where progress in understanding sophomore issues is being made is in the attention these issues are receiving from professional groups in both the nonprofit and for-profit sectors. We are seeing an increase in preconference workshops and sessions offered at national conferences, such as those hosted by the National Resource Center for The First-Year Experience and Students in Transition, the National Academic Advising Association, and the National Association of Student Personnel Administrators. Teleconferences and web-based seminars on sophomore issues offered by the Paperclips organization, the National Resource Center, and Noel-Levitz have been well attended. Sophomore listservs, national surveys, and articles about sophomore issues are beginning to flourish.

With the increased attention to sophomore issues among various professional groups, there also has been more of an intentional effort to collaborate between student and academic affairs units, as can be seen in conference presentations, campus initiatives, positions that are responsible for sophomore programming, and in research. This very monograph is a blend of these areas. The collaboration that is evident in successful sophomore initiatives is an excellent model for higher education as a whole.

However, some of the apparently simplest recommendations from our earlier monograph have proven to be the most difficult to implement. Despite the burgeoning interest and programming focused on sophomores, many of the initiatives have not been intentionally planned and assessed from their inception. The case study of Colorado College (chapter 5) provides a welcome exception to that trend. In addition, few sophomore programs have established strong links with the first-year programming on campus. Too often, the sophomore initiatives are not building on the strong foundation of the first-year experience but exist as isolated programs dependent on one or two key personnel, without whom the program would cease to exist. The model offered by Beloit College (chapter 4) offers a refreshing exception and is one upon which other colleges and universities can pattern their efforts.

Probably the most difficult recommendation from our earlier monograph was to pay more attention to the experiences of students in their second year at two-year institutions. While those colleges have gained an increasing amount of attention nationally over the past seven years, that attention has focused almost exclusively on matriculation to four-year institutions. The needs of the second-year student in a two-year college remain essentially unexplored. With nearly half of the college students in the nation enrolled in two-year colleges, the emphasis needs to be on far more than the transition of the second-year student to a four-year institution.

Finally, we ended our earlier monograph with an exhortation to increase sophomores' academic engagement in order to maintain the momentum of the first year. But as Molly Schaller notes in chapter 1, sophomores are in considerable transition intellectually. As a result, any attempts to increase academic engagement cannot be "one-size-fits-all" but rather must take into consideration the cognitive development and motivation level of the individual student. Gansemer-Topf, Stern, and Benjamin (chapter 3) poignantly highlight the academic issues experienced by sophomores. With so many sophomore-level courses being large lecture sections and containing a wide variety of student ability levels and interests, the challenge of increased academic engagement is becoming more and more important to meeting the needs of students in their second year.

Meaning, purpose, engagement, direction, and support are some of the issues highlighted throughout this monograph, bringing to light the campus programs and initiatives that represent the latest thinking on the complex needs of students in their second year of college. Collectively, the models and theories described provide readers with a much-needed update on the challenges and opportunities facing our students in this important transition year. Moreover, we hope this work inspires institutions to continue (or to begin) transforming the second college year so that sophomores experience increasing levels of learning and success.

References

Gardner, J. N., Pattengale, J., & Schreiner, L. A. (2000). The sophomore year: Summary and recommendations. In L. A. Schreiner & J. Pattengale (Eds.), *Visible solutions for invisible students: Helping sophomores succeed* (Monograph No. 31, pp. 89-93). Columbia, SC: University of South Carolina, National Resource Center for The First-Year Experience & Students in Transition.

Schreiner, L. A., & Pattengale, J. (Eds.). (2000). *Visible solutions for invisible students: Helping sophomores succeed* (Monograph No. 31). Columbia, SC: University of South Carolina, National Resource Center for The First-Year Experience & Students in Transition.

Introduction

Barbara F. Tobolowsky & Stephanie K. Serven

In early 2005, the Center staff was one year away from celebrating the 25th year of our Annual Conference on The First-Year Experience. We were happy to see from our listservs and conference presentations that many institutions had institutionalized their first-year efforts and were seeing positive results. More first-year students were taking first-year seminars and participating in other first-year initiatives. Most important, these students were being retained at greater levels, earning more credits, and doing better academically than students who did not participate in such programs. Though we continued to hear from people eager to improve or begin first-year efforts, we noticed that we were also hearing more frequently from educators who were worried about their second-year students, who appeared to be floundering. Did these students who felt well supported in the first year somehow feel left in the dark as sophomores?

A new dialogue was developing, and we saw it first hand. At both the 2004 and 2005 Students in Transition conferences, Julie Stockenberg from Colorado College and Ed Chan from Kennesaw State University facilitated roundtable discussions on the sophomore experience to packed rooms. Molly Schaller shared her research on sophomores in a session at the 2005 conference. At the same time, Brad Cox and Stephanie Serven developed the Center's web site devoted to sophomore programs—providing links to the few programs in existence. When we launched the web site, we were happy to have listed 20 programs. The number has almost doubled since then, with more being added all the time. Then, in spring 2006, the Center offered a teleconference on the topic—*The Forgotten Student: Understanding and Supporting Sophomores*—featuring Marcia Baxter Magolda, Rajesh Bellani, and Ed Chan. We estimate almost 3,000 people at 136 sites participated in this teleconference. Clearly, this was an emerging area of interest, and people were eager to get help as they developed programs.

Although historically sophomore students have been overlooked, both on college campuses and in the higher education literature, there has long been an awareness that many students struggle during their second year of college. In fact, more than 50 years ago, Freedman (1956) described sophomores as experiencing a sense of inertia and disorganization. Subsequent research has both broadened and deepened the academy's understanding of second-year students. For example, Schaller (2005) describes sophomore students as "standing on a fence," a phrase that illustrates their indecision about where they stand in the context of their past and their future (p. 19). While they have had a year to become acclimated to the institution and collegiate life and to make connections with faculty, staff, and other students, most have not yet declared a course of study or determined what they will do after college.

During the second college year, many students also begin to recognize discrepancies between their expectations and the realities of college, contributing to their feelings of uncertainty about the future (Evenbeck, Boston, DuVivier, & Hallberg, 2000; Gardner, 2000). Simply put, many sophomores seem to drift through their second year of college (Gardner), overwhelmed, unengaged, and seemingly uninterested in their academic pursuits. These difficulties and feelings are hallmarks of the "sophomore slump," a time in which students struggle to establish themselves as individuals, find their passions and develop a personal worldview, determine what they want to get out of college, and establish short- and long-term goals (Gardner, Pattengale, & Schreiner, 2000; Lemons & Richmond, 1987; Margolis, 1976).

Despite growing awareness of sophomore-student issues, institutions have typically allocated their scarce resources to helping students mediate other college transitions (i.e., transitions from high school to college and from college to the working world). Significantly, it is only recently that institutions have begun to recognize the need to address sophomore issues, having watched sophomore students achieve lower GPAs (Gardner et al., 2000; Pattengale, 2000; Pattengale & Schreiner, 2000), depart the university (Freedman, 1956; Noel & Levitz, 1991; Richmond & Lemons, 1987), or simply disengage and float passively through the remainder of their college years.

Nevertheless, a focus on sophomore issues was not a totally new area of interest for those in our network or for the Center. In fact, we published a monograph edited by Laurie Schreiner and Jerry Pattengale entitled *Visible Solutions for Invisible Students: Helping Sophomores Succeed* in 2000. This monograph was an attempt to define the needs and concerns of sophomore students, outline existing efforts to serve this student population, and make recommendations for helping these students succeed. What we discovered then—and what continues to be largely true—is that there is a dearth of empirical evidence on the experiences of second-year students and the programs designed to serve them.

While *Visible Solutions* remains a valuable resource for educators interested in second-year student programming, the number of people seeking help and eager to discuss this student population has continued to grow since its publication. We felt it was important to try to capture what was going on in second-year programs today. Therefore, the Center started developing an instrument to study the status of second-year initiatives. We were eager to find out what was happening at the national level with second-year programs. Who administered them? Were they being assessed and what were the outcomes of that assessment? This instrument was different from the one we used to find out about first-year seminars in that we were not investigating a single curricular offering. Rather, we wanted to gain a sense of the range of initiatives intentionally designed for second-year students. After months of developing and piloting an instrument, we conducted the study in fall 2005 with the intent of publishing our findings in monograph form.

While we were conducting our survey research, we put out a call for institutional representatives to tell us about assessed sophomore initiatives on their campuses with the goal of creating a second monograph devoted to sharing these case studies. We were disappointed that so few institutions responded—too few, in fact, to warrant a complete monograph. Why? Were too few initiatives in existence? Were sophomore-specific efforts so new that no one had assessed them? We can only guess at the reasons. However, we thank those institutions that responded to our call. We use their programs as examples in chapter 8.

Another experience also affected the development of this monograph. In June 2006, senior staff members from the Center joined a number of other educators interested in second-year students at a Sophomore Summit hosted by Rajesh Bellani and Kim Taylor at Colgate University. Meeting with individuals who shared an interest in understanding and supporting this group of students was an inspiring experience. Some of the participants had established programs, others were researching the population, and others were seeking answers. The meeting was so stimulating that the Center staff who attended felt that this monograph needed to capture the work of some of these individuals in order to provide the most current and comprehensive portrait of the sophomore experience available.

The resulting monograph is a convergence of these three projects and opens with Molly Schaller, one of the primary thinkers and researchers on this population, providing insight into sophomore student development issues. Chapter 2 describes the findings of the Center's National Survey on Sophomore Initiatives. In chapter 3, Ann Gansemer-Topf and her colleagues share findings from their in-depth study of sophomore students at Grinnell College. This work is a wonderful complement to the national profile, because it allows us to get a better understanding of the second college year from the students' perspectives. The remaining chapters of the monograph provide some excellent examples of work being done for sophomores from some of the individuals who attended that Sophomore Summit in June 2006. These examples span from relatively new to well-established programs, from programs with significant funding to those that are cobbling together support from a variety of areas. For example, Bill Flanagan describes initiatives at Beloit College, which has, perhaps, the longest-running programs for sophomores. Beloit's sophomore retreat, for instance, has been in existence for 15 years. This is followed by the work Julie Stockenberg has done at Colorado College in identifying existing initiatives and repackaging them as a coordinated effort supported by a generous budget. Ed Chan shares information about programs at Kennesaw State University, where there is interest in sophomore initiatives, but limited financial resources. Finally, Kim Taylor and Rajesh Bellani share information about Colgate University's comprehensive efforts, supported by the Mellon Foundation, that focus on civic engagement in the sophomore year. The final chapter of the monograph culls lessons learned from all these examples and from the Center's research to provide some suggestions on how readers might develop and/or expand their own efforts in support of sophomores. We hope this monograph helps provide guidance to educators interested in second-year students and moves the dialogue forward so that these students are no longer left in the dark.

References

Evenbeck, S. E., Boston, M., DuVivier, R. S., & Hallberg, K. (2000). Institutional approaches to helping sophomores. In L. A. Schreiner & J. Pattengale (Eds.), *Visible solutions for invisible students: Helping sophomores succeed* (Monograph No. 31, pp. 79-87). Columbia, SC: University of South Carolina, National Resource Center for The First-Year Experience and Students in Transition.

Freedman, M. B. (1956). The passage through college. *Journal of Social Issues, 12*(4), 13-28.

Gardner, J. N., Pattengale, J., & Schreiner, L. A. (2000). Summary and recommendations. In L. A. Schreiner & J. Pattengale (Eds.), *Visible solutions for invisible students: Helping sophomores succeed* (Monograph No. 31, pp. 89-93). Columbia, SC: University of South Carolina, National Resource Center for The First-Year Experience and Students in Transition.

Gardner, P. D. (2000). From drift to engagement: Finding purpose and making career connections in the sophomore year. In L. A. Schreiner & J. Pattengale (Eds.), *Visible solutions for invisible students: Helping sophomores succeed* (Monograph No. 31, pp. 67-77). Columbia, SC: University of South Carolina, National Resource Center for The First-Year Experience and Students in Transition.

Lemons, L. J., & Richmond, D. R. (1987, Winter). A developmental perspective of sophomore slump. *NASPA Journal, 24* (3), 15-19.

Margolis, G. (1976). Unslumping our sophomores: Some clinical observations and strategies. *Journal of American College Health, 25*, 133-136.

Noel, L., & Levitz, R. (1991, November). Beating the sophomore slump. *Recruitment & Retention in Higher Education,* 1-3.

Pattengale, J. (2000). Policies and practices to enhance sophomore success. In L. A. Schreiner & J. Pattengale (Eds.), *Visible solutions for invisible students: Helping sophomores succeed* (Monograph No. 31, pp. 31-45). Columbia, SC: University of South Carolina, National Resource Center for The First-Year Experience and Students in Transition.

Pattengale, J. & Schreiner, L. A. (2000). What is the sophomore slump and why should we care? In L. A. Schreiner & J. Pattengale (Eds.), *Visible solutions for invisible students: Helping sophomores succeed* (Monograph No. 31, pp. 31-45). Columbia, SC: University of South Carolina, National Resource Center for The First-Year Experience and Students in Transition.

Richmond, D. R., & Lemons, L. J. (1985). Sophomore slump: An individual approach to recognition and response. *Journal of College Student Personnel, 26*(2), 176-177.

Schaller, M. A. (2005, July-August). Wandering and wondering: Traversing the uneven terrain of the second college year. *About Campus, 10*, 17-24.

Schreiner, L. A., & Pattengale, J. (Eds). (2000). *Visible solutions for invisible students: Helping sophomores succeed* (Monograph No. 31). Columbia, SC: University of South Carolina, National Resource Center for The First-Year Experience and Students in Transition.

Chapter 1

The Development of College Sophomores

Molly A. Schaller

In American higher education, professionals work diligently to shape an experience that maximizes the positive impact on college students and, thus, upon society. While the tide of discussion is changing from that of the development of the whole student to a more context-specific discussion of student engagement (Manning, Kinzie, & Schuh, 2006), student development theories can help frame our understanding of a particular group or student experience and are, thus, a suitable starting place for discussing the sophomore experience. Many have chronicled the lack of attention paid to college sophomores (Feldman & Newcomb, 1969; Flanagan, 1991; Lemons & Richmond, 1987; Morgan & Davis, 1981), and findings suggest college sophomores go to school each year and either persist or leave depending upon their experience. In large measure, this experience has gone unstudied. Focus on the first-year experience, both in research and in practice, has taken priority. The success of first-year experience initiatives have been so pronounced on many campuses that the questions of persistence and retention of sophomore students has naturally arisen. This chapter provides an introduction to understanding the student experience in the sophomore year by examining related theoretical perspectives.

This chapter explores two large categories of student development theory. Psychosocial theories are those that explore the development of a sense of self in relationship to society and societal expectations. Identity development is often the central focus of this developmental task. Cognitive developmental theories, the second category, explore how individuals make sense of knowledge, how they understand the world, and how they make meaning. Transition theory and literature on the sophomore slump are also reviewed because they are especially relevant to the sophomore experience. Transition theory provides insight into how individuals negotiate major life transitions, especially those that cause individuals to examine their position in the world, their notion of self, and their future. This body of theory is particularly applicable to college students and can provide specific insight into the sophomore experience. Sophomore slump literature from the 1970s and 1980s attempted to explain the phenomenon that professionals reported seeing in second-year students. Finally, this chapter provides a specific theory related to traditional-age sophomore students.

While theory can provide a framework for making sense of students' experiences, it should be viewed as only one important source of insight into those experiences. Institution-specific assessment measures can provide a more accurate picture of a specific phenomenon or student experience. Nothing replaces listening to and seeking understanding of the individual student.

Developmental Theories

For many students, enrollment in college coincides with "finding oneself" or figuring out what one wants to do with life. The new relationships, new knowledge, and exposure to diverse ways of thinking challenge individuals to determine who they are and what they want for their futures. Developmental theory provides a framework for understanding how students, in this case sophomore students, negotiate these changes in their lives. The two major views of student development theory that seem most appropriate to understanding the experience of sophomores are the psychosocial and cognitive-developmental perspectives.

Psychosocial Development

Psychosocial developmental theories provide insight into the "content of development" (Evans, Forney, & Guido-DiBrito, 1998, p. 32) or student examinations of their current and future lives, definitions of self, the importance of relationships, personal beliefs, and future directions. Much of the knowledge of college students' personal development is based on Erikson's theory of psychosocial development. Erikson highlighted "identity versus role confusion" as the central developmental task of the traditional-age college student (Pascarella & Terenzini, 1991). Chickering (1969), and later Chickering and Reisser (1993), applied Erikson's notion of identity development to the college-age population, expanding our understanding of the college student experience. Chickering and Reisser described seven vectors of development. While none are specifically the focus of the sophomore year, each vector has implications for second-year students.

Competence. Achieving competence, according to Chickering and Reisser (1993), is a "three-tined pitchfork" (p. 53). The three tines are intellectual competence, physical or manual competence, and social or interpersonal competence. Chickering and Reisser stated that the accomplishment of each type of competence has impact on one's readiness to take risks and to try new things, while feeling comfortable with peers. New students experience a decline in competence during the first college year, which may indicate that sophomore students begin the second year still attempting to manage some competence issues.

Managing emotions. Chickering and Reisser (1993) stated that development along this vector involves first becoming aware of one's emotions, including having the ability to differentiate between feelings. Second, they suggested that once individuals are able to distinguish between emotions they then learn to gauge the intensity of their feelings. Third, the individual must determine if his/her emotions are self-nurturing or toxic. In moving along this vector, Chickering and Reisser asserted, individuals begin to learn the source of their emotions, to value the information that emotions provide, and to understand the consequences for emotional outbursts. Most students negotiate these challenges during the first two years of their college education. Students begin to use flexible control over their emotions as they gain independence in the college setting.

Moving through autonomy toward interdependence. Becoming autonomous is dependent upon one's ability to have both emotional and instrumental independence (Chickering & Reisser, 1993). The student must be able to stand alone and provide for his or her own emotional needs. Additionally, the student develops an ability to carry out activities and to handle problems as they arise. Interdependence is the end state to becoming autonomous, where rewarding relationships are defined by the give and take between individuals. Chickering and Reisser cited numerous studies that show an increase in autonomy during the four years of college. However, they suggested that there might be a decrease in autonomy during the first sophomore term, which may suggest that students reconnect with home and family after they have pulled away during the first year.

Developing mature interpersonal relationships. One's ability to develop mature interpersonal relationships marks a shift in the quality of relationships in which an individual chooses to engage (Chickering & Reisser, 1993). In this process, individuals develop a tolerance and appreciation of differences and a capacity for true intimacy. Movement along this vector indicates a decrease in ethnocentricity, toward an acceptance and celebration of differences found in others. It also indicates a growing openness and empathy toward others, which leaves one more open to deep interpersonal connections. Chickering and Reisser cite research suggesting students develop mature interpersonal relationships during the college years.

Establishing identity. Miller and Winston (1990) defined Chickering's identity vector as "...confidence in one's ability to maintain inner sameness and continuity" (p. 104). Chickering and Reisser (1993) later defined the vector as having a solid sense of self and an inner feeling of mastery and ownership. This vector involves a number of complex tasks that one must accomplish, including developing a sense of comfort with one's body and appearance, gender, sexual orientation, and lifestyle; accepting one's social, historical, and cultural background; establishing a sense of personal stability and integration; and gaining an overall sense of self-acceptance and self-esteem.

Jones and McEwen (2000) asserted that one's identity involves multiple dimensions of race, culture, gender, sexual orientation, religion, and social class. Research examines the differing experiences of many of these dimensions separately; however, Jones and McEwen suggest that it is the unique experience of each individual based upon a set of personal characteristics and within a certain context where developmental challenges exist.

Developing purpose. Chickering and Reisser (1993) stated that if the vector of developing identity was a function of deciding "Who am I?" (p. 209), then developing purpose involves answering the question "Where am I going?" (p. 209). Movement in this area involves the development of a set of priorities that integrate one's vocational plans, personal interests, and interpersonal and family relationships. While development along this vector occurs throughout the four years, many consider the selection of and commitment to a major as signs of clear movement toward developing purpose.

Developing integrity. Developing integrity can be defined as the development of congruence between one's behaviors and values toward a sense of responsibility for self and others, and the ability to thoughtfully apply ethical principles in one's life (Chickering & Reisser, 1993). Movement along this vector involves an increase in care for human kind and the ownership of values based on what one believes, instead of what one is told to believe. Developing integrity, like developing purpose, is said to follow the development of one's identity, and thus is often an issue for students later in their college experience.

Understanding Sophomores Through Psychosocial Development

A great deal of research focuses on the psychosocial development of college students, yet none of this research has attempted to specifically describe the development of traditional-age sophomore students. In their summary of research on the impact of college on students, Pascarella and Terenzini (2005) reported that evidence suggests that college students experience growth in autonomy, locus of control, self-efficacy, social competence, leadership skills, and personal development during the college years. In the absence of specific findings regarding sophomore students, a number of authors have translated current research to the sophomore experience.

Regarding identity development, Furr and Gannaway (1982) suggested that sophomore students may experience intensified conflicts over identity, in part due to the pressure to make decisions about career plans, values, and lifestyle preferences. Lemons and Richmond (1987) looked to Chickering's theory to understand the sophomore experience. They inferred from Chickering that second-year students could be dealing with issues of competence, autonomy, identity, and developing a sense of purpose. According to Lemons and Richmond, sophomore students may experience increasing insecurity as they come to understand the expectations of friends, parents, and self but are unclear about how they can meet all of these expectations. Sophomores may also struggle with autonomy as they experience frustration over their inability to break financial ties with parents. Lemons and Richmond suggested that problems with competence and autonomy stifle the development of identity, which is particularly troubling for students dealing with the deadline of selecting a major by the end of the sophomore year.

Hood, Riahinejad, and White (1986) used Erwin's Identity Scale (EIS), which combines Chickering's and Erikson's views, to look at changes in identity during the college years. In this study, first-year students took the EIS during the middle and end of their first year, then during the second semester of their sophomore year and again in the senior year. On the EIS scales, most of the change occurred during the sophomore through senior years. Loeb and Magee (1992) found that students' reported self-esteem, self-confidence, and intelligence all decreased significantly after the start of college. They reported that by the end of the sophomore year most students' self-perception recovered. They suggest that, "perhaps it is necessary to fall back, to lose some bravado, to experience doubt and conflict before one can experience growth" (p. 354).

Loevinger et al. (1985), Greeley and Tinsley (1988), and Hood et al. (1986), each found an increasing sense of identity during the early college years. Loevinger and her co-authors reported that there were decreases in ego development at the beginning of the college career followed by a rebound. This longitudinal study was particularly important because it challenged the conventional notion that individuals only move forward in ego development. Greeley and Tinsley found differences across gender in ego development at the beginning of college. However, none of these studies shows a clear pattern of change or growth. In fact, on some scales, some groups showed increases in development during the sophomore year while other groups exhibited decreases.

Cognitive Development Models

Intellectual development. Many theorists have studied intellectual development from birth through the college years. The work of two theorists, William Perry and Marcia Baxter Magolda, is particularly applicable here, because sophomores have been studied in light of their theories.

Perry (1968) studied college students during the 1950s and early 1960s and subsequently created a developmental scheme to describe students. Perry's theory has since been used to understand how students view knowledge. Perry defined nine positions of reasoning. Position 1, dualism, is the view that there is always a right and wrong answer in the world. Position 2, multiplicity pre-legitimate, is the view that any diversity in answers is a mistake or a test. Position 3, multiplicity subordinate, is the view that not all questions in the world have an answer, but this state is temporary. Position 4, multiplism correlate or relativism subordinate, is the view that the diversity of answers or uncertainty is the norm, so any view can be legitimate. Position 5, relativism, is the view that knowledge is contextual and relativistic, so answers to life questions can be weighed based on evidence and the support for a given argument. Positions 6 through 9 do not involve a different cognitive perspective beyond relativism, rather they address the style of commitment beyond relativism.

Rodgers (1990) noted that most first-year students score at Perry position 2, between position 2 and 3, or at position 3, suggesting that the sophomore student could be at any number of positions. Students who are between position 2 and 3 may just be beginning to have questions about some long held "truths." This leads to position 3 where students acknowledge there are not clear answers for all life questions, even if this uncertainty is temporary. Furr and Gannaway (1982) asserted that Perry's perspective on intellectual development suggests that sophomores may be at a level that makes it difficult to deal with the complexities of college living.

Baxter Magolda (1992) conducted an in-depth longitudinal study of traditional-age college students. Through this study, she developed the model of epistemological reflection, which contains four different knowledge perspectives: (a) the absolute knower, (b) the transitional knower, (c) the independent knower, and (d) the contextual knower. Those in the first three perspectives may use one of two gender-related patterns in the way that they approach knowing. Men in her study tended to use patterns that emphasized personal mastery while women tended to use patterns that emphasized relational knowing. The use of patterns seems to be fluid and not rigidly held by either gender.

Baxter Magolda (1992) found that absolute knowers view knowledge as certain. Knowledge exists and can be transferred from faculty or authority figures to the absolute knower. Absolute knowers may use a pattern of receiving or mastering knowledge. The receiving absolute knower approaches the attainment of knowledge with distance, seldom interacting with faculty, and other authority figures. Those who use a mastering pattern to gain knowledge are more likely to engage in debate and view the learning process as interactive. While neither pattern is wholly gender related, more women used the receiving pattern, while men were more likely to use the mastering pattern.

Transitional knowers, according to Baxter Magolda (1992) experience a shift in their view of knowledge. The process of gaining information no longer satisfies them; they wish to understand knowledge. There are two different patterns that emerged for transitional knowers. Those who used the interpersonal approach, mostly women, wanted to have interaction in the process of understanding knowledge. Through relationships with faculty and peers, those using this approach could understand better. Those using an impersonal approach, mostly men, were more likely to view learning as an individual endeavor.

Independent knowers view knowledge as uncertain and, therefore, view their own ideas as important (Baxter Magolda, 1992). Women were most likely to use an interindividual pattern when approaching knowledge, looking to interact with others and to share their views in the approach to knowledge. Individual pattern knowers, usually men, were interested in thinking for themselves. Baxter Magolda found very few students who exhibited contextual knowing. These students view knowledge as uncertain, but weigh arguments and evidence to determine better or worse answers.

First-year students are predominately absolute knowers, as are many sophomores (Baxter Magolda, 1992). In fact, 46% of sophomores in Baxter Magolda's study were absolute knowers, while 53% were transitional knowers and 1% were independent knowers (pp. 70-72). Sophomore students seem either to view knowledge as certain or seek to gain understanding. This nearly even split between absolute and transitional knowers illustrates the complexities in understanding the sophomore population. Table 1 reviews the characteristics of these two knowledge positions.

Table 1
Traditional-Age Sophomore Students' Intellectual Development

Absolute Knowers		Transitional Knowers	
Receiving Pattern	Mastering Pattern	Interpersonal Pattern	Impersonal Pattern
• Student looks to authority figure to guide learning and to gain information. • Peers help to make atmosphere relaxed and to ask questions of authority figure.	• Student seeks to show authority figure their interest and mastery of material. • Peers debate and test each other for knowledge acquisition.	• Uncertainty becomes real. • Learning becomes important. • Peers provide exposure to new views. • Student seeks interaction with authority.	• Student seeks to understand rather than memorize. • Expands views via debate with others. • Uncertainty is resolved via logic and reason.

Source. Baxter Magolda, 1992.

Both Perry and Baxter Magolda point to a shift in the view of knowledge during the sophomore year. Those sophomore students who are in multiplicity pre-legitimate or are absolute knowers will accept the views of "good authorities." Those sophomores who are in multiplicity-subordinate or transitional knowing will begin to question authorities and seek to understand what they are being taught.

Moral development. Another area of developmental theory that is useful in understanding sophomore students is their moral reasoning, or the manner in which individuals define moral values and make moral decisions. Moral development was studied at length by Lawrence Kohlberg (1969), who originally studied the moral reasoning of adolescent males. Kohlberg described three levels of moral development, each with two stages. At level 1 or the Preconventional level, moral reasoning is characterized as a concern for self. In stage 1, the individual works to avoid punishment or to gain rewards. In stage 2, the individual makes decisions in his or her own best interest, avoiding punishment or gaining rewards. Level 2 or the Conventional level is characterized by moral decisions that are made in light of other's views. In stage 3, the individual makes decisions in order to gain approval from others, attempting to be viewed as good by others. In stage 4, the individual makes decisions with concern for issues of law and order. Level 3 or Postconventional reasoning is based on a set of universal principles that guide moral decisions. In stage 5, moral decisions are those that promote fundamental human rights. In stage 6, the individual makes decisions based on universal principles, which can be generalized for all situations.

Research shows a significant growth in moral development from the first college year to senior year (Pascarella & Terenzini, 2005). Yet, Kohlberg and Kramer (1969) found a regression in moral development for sophomores, to below stage 4. This regression may in fact be a necessary developmental step in continuing growth. Students may be overwhelmed by the disequilibrium produced through changing approaches to moral reasoning. Individuals may seek equilibrium through regression when developmental changes are dramatic or drastic. Cohen (1982) looked at the moral development of students in Greek-letter organizations. In studying fraternity and sorority students, Cohen found that sophomore students were slightly below stage 4 and had in fact regressed from their first-year position. Later, Kilgannon and Erwin (1992) studied the moral development of Greek students through a longitudinal study. They found that moral development is higher at the end of the sophomore year for non-Greek women than for Greek women and for both Greek and non-Greek men, showing that students' experiences and gender may play a role in their moral development.

Sophomore students, then, are likely to use stage 3 moral reasoning that allows them to gain the approval of others, including friends, roommates, and other peers (Table 2). Or, sophomore students may use stage 4 moral reasoning, where they attempt to uphold consistent laws established by society as a duty they have to the greater good (Evans et al., 1998).

Table 2
Moral Reasoning in Sophomore Students

Conventional Moral Reasoning	
Stage 3	Stage 4
• Moral choices are based upon being viewed positively by others. Peers and parents play a key role in student's choices. • Students seek to meet the expectations of those around them.	• Students begin to recognize the value of law and order to maintaining social order. • Laws and rules that provide for the protection or maintenance of groups/society are valued.

Source. Adapted from Kohlberg, 1969.

Transition Theory

Transition, according to Bridges (1980) is the "...natural process of disorientation and reorientation that marks the turning points of the path of growth" (p. 5). This natural process occurs, Bridges asserted, constantly in American society. Our view of life and the complexities of our society challenge us to make constant choices about our lives. These choices can become turning points in our lives, and all turning points are disorienting.

Levinson (1986) identified the ages of 17 to 22 as the "Early Adult Transition," a developmental period in which pre-adulthood draws to a close and the era of early adulthood gets underway. Levinson described this time as a "new step in individuation" (p. 5) where the individual modifies relationships with family and the world as he or she becomes a part of the adult world.

The Early Adult Transition

According to Levinson (1978) two major tasks face the individual in the early adult transition. First, the individual leaves the pre-adult world. Second, the individual creates a new and stable structure for adulthood. Most traditional-aged college sophomores are 19 or 20 years old during their sophomore year. Thus, Levinson would suggest that most college sophomores will be in the beginning or middle part of this transition phase.

Leaving the Pre-Adult World

Many college students experience the beginning of college in the same way that Levinson (1978) described the beginning of the early adult transition. Students begin their transition to college by moving away from home or as Levinson put it, separating from their family of origin. During this portion of the transition, students may become less financially dependent upon their parents. Many will take on loans and employment to finance their education. Many will also enter new roles and living arrangements that are more autonomous and include increased levels of responsibility. For many first-year students this includes a variety of choices perhaps not available during the high school years. Students who move away to college must decide when to wake up and when to go to bed, what to eat, which classes to attend, how to care for personal belongings, how to do the laundry, and how to handle medical concerns. College students may also be dealing with a new found freedom that allows them to make personal choices about the use of alcohol or other drugs, sexual activity, religious beliefs, and choices about their appearance. There may be, for these students, an increasing differentiation between the student and parents.

As Flanagan (1991) pointed out, the sophomore year may be particularly difficult because the newness of college has worn off. Sophomores face at least three years of hard work in front of them, with increasing financial burdens over the first year. At the same time, these students may be struggling to determine career goals and to deal with personal development issues.

The Transition Process

Transition theorists seem to describe most transitions as a three-step process. For Bridges (1980), this process involves an ending, a neutral zone, and a new beginning. Similarly, Keleman (1979) describes the transition process as involving an ending, a middle ground, and a beginning.

Endings. Bridges (1980) stated that the ending process involves a disengagement that is the beginning of the transition. Frey and Carlock (1984) suggested that transitions may be either internally or externally induced. Bridges suggested that events pile up, and individuals respond inwardly in ways that leave them changed. Transitions force individuals to look at the negative and positive sides of life situations (Bridges). Through this examination, individuals deconstruct their past definitions of self but have yet to construct a new definition of self.

The neutral zone. The middle stage of the transition process involves a time of disorganization according to Keleman (1979). Bridges (1980) described this time as a moratorium. The individual in transition finds new ways of being alone and away from all the familiar distractions of life. This can be, Bridges asserted, an opportunity to expand one's sense of reality. This stage of the transition, however, involves an emptiness that is essential in the process. Bridges stated that emptiness provides those in transition with perspective on the stages of life, one not possible at any other time in life.

Beginnings. New beginnings are internal, rather than external (Bridges, 1980) and may bring with them different levels of change. For example, Frey and Carlock (1984) defined high-risk changes as those that are initiated by a significant loss rather than new opportunities or other positive experiences. The beginning process may then involve more or less dramatic changes. Schlossberg and Kent (1979) suggested that environment makes a difference in the transition process. Support systems, intimate relationships, a strong network of friends, and a cohesive and adaptable family can play important roles in sustaining a person through transition.

The Sophomore Slump

Feldman and Newcomb (1969) defined the sophomore slump as a time of student dissatisfaction with the college and with self. While the term has been used in higher education for decades, little research has been conducted on the sophomore slump. A number of authors have attempted to describe the phenomenon, but none have actually measured its existence. In their summary of existing definitions, Lemons and Richmond (1987) characterized sophomore slump as a time of identity crisis involving the social, academic, and personal self, as well as, a period of confusion and uncertainty during the sophomore year.

In an attempt to provide sophomores with special services, Morgan and Davis (1981) discussed what sophomores were experiencing with other professionals. Student service professionals believed that sophomore students felt alone on campus. In fact, Morgan and Davis reported that sophomores might experience a period of rejection as institutions neglect their needs in order to attend to the issues of first-year students. The focus on the first year suggests that sophomores lose their identity as a special class within the institution. Today, such perceptions may be even more pronounced because institutions have worked hard to develop comprehensive first-year experience programs. In his study on retention efforts, Flanagan (1991) noted that, "The sophomore year is likely to be the time when students find they cannot obtain the courses, housing, financial aid, or type of academic advising and institutional attention they may have received as freshmen" (p. 5).

Sophomore Student Issues

Upcraft, Gardner, and Barefoot (2005) identified a set of developmental tasks that first-year students should address. These include (a) developing intellectual and academic competence, (b) establishing and maintaining interpersonal relationships, (c) exploring identity development, (d) deciding on a career, (e) maintaining health and wellness, and (f) considering faith and the spiritual dimensions of life, (g) developing multicultural awareness, and (h) developing civic responsibility. Few would suggest that first-year students actually complete these tasks by the end of the first year—or in some cases, the end of college. Yet, practitioners and researchers can use these developmental goals from the first year as goals for the sophomore year and beyond.

Schaller (2005) engaged traditional-age sophomore students in a qualitative study to better understand how they interpreted the sophomore-year experience. While her study was limited in scope, her findings provide some insight into the manner in which the challenges described by Upcraft et al. (2005) are experienced beyond the first year. Schaller described a four-stage model that her sophomore participants moved through including random exploration, focused exploration, tentative choices, and commitment.

Random Exploration

In the initial experience of college, Schaller (2005) suggested that students engage in significant exploration of themselves, their relationships, and the academic setting. In random exploration, students make few active choices about their lives; instead, they seem to fall into decisions that are convenient. They move haphazardly through the key choices faced by first-year students. Students may remain in random exploration through the beginning of the sophomore year or move to the next stage as early as the middle of the first year.

Focused Exploration

The pressures of the sophomore year seem to come into plain view for many students over the summer between the first and second years (Schaller, 2005). The requirement to decide upon majors combined with an opportunity to reflect on the first-year choices seems to propel students into a new approach to decision making. No longer haphazard, students in Schaller's study seemed to become deeply concerned about decisions in their lives, specifically about their major and future academic direction, their friendships and relationships, and their definition of self. While Chickering and Reisser (1993) suggested that the process of developing purpose was a primary focus after major identity issues are settled, the structure of academia pushes decisions onto students who are still negotiating key identity issues.

Students who remain in focused exploration for long periods of time without resolving the key decisions regarding self-definition, selection of key relationships, and future direction seemed to be at greatest risk for high levels of frustration and anxiety (Schaller, 2005). Schaller suggested that when students begin to settle some decisions or at least move into the next stage of tentative choices, in one area of their lives, they could use these decisions as a foundation for the remaining pending decisions. However, the amount of time students experience indecision increases the pressure to make choices. In some ways, this can be counterproductive to the identity development process. Students may begin to make choices that are easy, convenient, or nearly appropriate for the self if they cannot sustain focused exploration. Some students seem to be more efficient in the exploration process. This may be because they have had many different life experiences to provide ample choices or because they have learned how to limit or select choices that are most appropriate for the self.

Tentative Choices

As students make initial choices, they begin to feel more comfortable about their lives. They describe themselves as more mature and responsible (Schaller, 2005); however, tentative choices is not a stage of complete certainty. Students may not remain with the initial choices that they make during this stage. They may continue to refine their choices as they gain new knowledge about themselves and the world around them. Most of the sophomores in Schaller's original study were in the tentative choices stage in at least one of the major areas of their lives (i.e., self, relationships, academic/future). This may be in response to the academic cycle and the requirement that students know their major prior to entering upper-level courses. It may be that sophomores conducted appropriate exploration processes or that the exploration process became tedious and tiresome, so students settled in their decision making.

Commitment

Schaller (2005) described commitment as a stage of security and certainty. Sophomores in this stage, while few in number, expressed high levels of confidence in their sense of self. They became involved in activities to secure their future. They began to limit relationships that were detrimental or that interfered with the relationships they valued most. They were the most able to describe themselves and felt good about where they were as developing people.

If sophomores transition out of random exploration and into focused exploration sometime during the academic year, then they are in the midst of facing major decisions in their life regarding their sense of self, their view of learning, and their future. Supporting students in the move toward tentative choices and eventually commitment is not a simple task. It requires that students stay in the search, engage in self-reflection, and fully explore their options for a life direction.

Summary

As we begin to search for ways to serve sophomore students, a number of important questions about the sophomore year remain. Are there specific differences in the sophomore-year experience for different student groups? Is the experience of sophomores in the two-year college setting significantly or qualitatively different from that of students at four-year institutions? Are there certain contexts that do a better job of supporting students in negotiating the demands of the sophomore year? Each of these questions highlights important areas of future research as American higher education begins to pay close attention to sophomore students.

References

Baxter Magolda, M.B. (1992). *Knowing and reasoning in college*. San Francisco: Jossey-Bass.

Bridges, W. (1980). *Transitions: Making sense of life's changes*. Reading, MA: Addison-Wesley.

Chickering, A. W. (1969). *Education and identity*. San Francisco: Jossey-Bass.

Chickering, A. W., & Reisser, L. (1993). *Education and identity* (2nd ed.). San Francisco: Jossey-Bass.

Cohen, E. R. (1982). Using the defining issues test to assess stage of moral development among sorority and fraternity members. *Journal of College Student Development, 23*, 324-328.

Evans, N., Forney, D., & Guido-DiBrito, F. (1998). *Student development in college: Theory, research and practice.* San Francisco: Jossey-Bass.

Feldman, K. A., & Newcomb, T. M. (1969). *The impact of college on students.* Washington, DC: Jossey-Bass.

Flanagan, W. (1991). *Sophomore retention: The missing strategy in small college retention efforts* (Doctoral dissertation, University of Wisconsin-Madison, 1991). UMI No. 911372.

Frey, D., & Carlock, C. (1984). *Enhancing self-esteem*. Muncie, IN: Accelerated Press.

Furr, S. R., & Gannaway, L. (1982). Easing the sophomore slump: A student development approach. *Journal of College Student Personnel, 23*, 340-341.

Greeley, A. T., & Tinsley, H. E. (1988). Autonomy and intimacy development in college students: Sex difference and predictors. *Journal of College Student Development, 29*, 512-520.

Hood, A. B., Riahinejad, A. R., & White, D. B. (1986). Changes in ego identity during the college years. *Journal of College Student Personnel, 27*, 107-113.

Jones, S., & McEwen, M. (2000). A conceptual model of multiple dimensions of identity. *Journal of College Student Development, 41,* 405-414.

Keleman, S. (1979). *Somantic reality*. Berkeley, CA: Center Press.

Kilgannon, S. M., & Erwin, T. D. (1992). A longitudinal study about the identity and moral development of Greek students. *Journal of College Student Development, 33*, 253-259.

Kohlberg, L. (1969). Stage and sequence: The cognitive development approach to socialization. In D. A. Goslin (Ed.), *Handbook of socialization theory and research* (pp. 347-480). Chicago: Rand McNally.

Kohlberg, L., & Kramer, R. (1969). Continuities and discontinuities in childhood and adult moral development. *Human Development, 12*, 93-120.

Lemons, L. J., & Richmond, D. R. (1987). A developmental perspective of sophomore slump. *NASPA Journal*, 24, 15-19.

Levinson, D. (1978). *The seasons of a man's life*. New York: Knopf.

Levinson, D. (1986). A conception of adult development. *American Psychologist, 41*, 3-13.

Loeb, R. C., & Magee, P. M. (1992). Changes in attitudes and self-perceptions during the first two years of college. *Journal of College Student Development, 33*, 348-355.

Loevinger, J., Cohn, L. D., Bonneville, L. P., Redmore, C. D., Streich, D. D., & Sargent, M. (1985). Ego development in college. *Journal of Personality and Social Psychology, 48*, 947-962.

Manning, K., Kinzie, J., & Schuh, J. (2006). *One size does not fit all: Traditional and innovative models of student affairs practice*. New York, NY: Routledge.

Miller, T., & Winston, R., Jr. (1990). Assessing development from a psychosocial perspective. In D. Creamer & Associates (Eds.), *College student development theory and practice for the 1990s*. (ACPA Media Publication No. 49). Alexandria, VA: American College Personnel Association.

Morgan, J. D., & Davis, D. A. (1981). Sophomore students: They are special, too. *Journal of College Student Personnel, 22*, 170-171.

Pascarella, E. T., & Terenzini, P. T. (1991). *How college affects students*. San Francisco: Jossey-Bass.

Pascarella, E. T., & Terenzini, P. T. (2005). *How college affects students: A third decade of research*. San Francisco: Jossey-Bass.

Perry, W. G. (1968). *Forms of intellectual and ethical development in the college years: A scheme*. New York: Holt, Rinehart & Winston.

Rodgers, R. F. (1990). Recent theories and research underlying student development. In D. G. Creamer (Ed.), *College student development: Theory and practice for the 1990s* (pp. 27-279). Alexandria, VA: American College Personnel Association.

Schaller, M.A. (2005, July-August). Wandering and wondering: Traversing the uneven terrain of the second college year. *About Campus, 10*, 17-24.

Schlossberg, N., & Kent, L. (1979). Effective helping with women. In S. Eisenberg & L. Patterson (Eds.), *Helping clients with special concerns*. Chicago: Rand McNally.

Upcraft, M. L., Gardner, J. N., & Barefoot, B. O. (2005). *Challenging and supporting the first-year student: A handbook for improving the first year of college*. San Francisco: Jossey-Bass.

Chapter 2

Findings from the 2005 National Survey on Sophomore-Year Initiatives

Barbara F. Tobolowsky & Bradley E. Cox

In fall 2005, the National Resource Center for The First-Year Experience and Students in Transition administered a national survey to chief student affairs officers to get a better understanding of sophomore-specific efforts on four-year campuses. Though much of the Center's research efforts have been devoted to first-year programs, we have long been aware that student issues do not begin and end in the first year. It is essential that institutions have a better understanding of student challenges beyond the first year, so that they can provide the necessary supports for their students. This chapter focuses on the findings from our exploratory 2005 study providing a glimpse into what institutions are currently doing to assist their second-year students.

The National Resource Center conducted a study of second-year programs and initiatives at regionally accredited private and public four-year institutions (See appendix A for methodology). We had a response rate of 33.5% with 382 institutions participating in the survey. The findings from the survey provide baseline data regarding the most commonly offered initiatives or programs for sophomore students. After providing an overview of all initiatives, this chapter offers insight into specific efforts (i.e., advising, curricular offerings, mentoring, residential life, financial aid, events, publications), the administration of these efforts, related assessment data, and plans for the future initiatives.

Current Sophomore Initiatives

Overall, about one third (33.5%) of the responding institutions offered at least one initiative specifically or intentionally geared toward sophomores. Table 1 provides a snapshot of the types of sophomore initiatives most frequently found on the respondents' campuses.

Perhaps not surprisingly, most sophomore initiatives focus on career planning and the selection of a major. Considering that the sophomore year is the time during which many schools require students to select a major (Packard, 2004-05) and that the choice of a major has significant implications for the students' career choices, it seems appropriate that institutions have created mechanisms to assist sophomore students with these issues. In addition to advising functions, some initiatives focus on providing events for sophomores, service-learning opportunities, and less often, curricular offerings such as learning communities. Though some of these initiatives are not sophomore-specific and are available to all students, many are particularly geared to sophomores and may be part of a comprehensive, four-year program for students.

The survey did not ask the reason for these programmatic efforts, but a few institutions offered their rationales. For example, Oregon State University specifically targeted sophomores in this way to increase retention. Texas Tech University designed apartment-style housing to assist in the recruitment and retention of sophomore students. Therefore, for these institutions, and perhaps others, sophomore initiatives are directly linked to retention concerns.

Table 1
Institutions With Initiatives Specifically or Intentionally Geared Toward Sophomores

Initiative	Number	Percentage
Career planning	89	74.2
Programs to assist with selection of major	79	65.3
Academic advising	75	61.0
Class events (e.g., trips, dinners, dances)	56	46.3
Peer mentoring *by* sophomores (i.e., sophomore students mentoring other students)	54	46.2
Student government (e.g., sophomore council)	46	38.7
Residence life (e.g., sophomore-specific living arrangements)	40	33.6
Community service / service-learning	38	32.8
Faculty and staff mentors for sophomore students	37	31.4
Credit-bearing course (e.g., sophomore seminar)	24	21.1
Opportunities to co-teach or assist in teaching a class	24	20.7
Financial aid (e.g., sophomore scholarships, loans)	23	19.3
Cultural enrichment (e.g., plays, musical events, multicultural fairs)	22	18.8
Curricular learning communities (i.e., linked courses)	20	17.7
Publications for sophomores (e.g., sophomore newsletter or web site)	20	16.8
Peer mentoring *for* sophomores (i.e., students mentoring sophomores)	18	15.4
Other initiatives (n = 77)	22	28.6

Note. Ns for each initiative type ranged from 113 to 123 (of the 128 institutions with at least one initiative). Percentages reported are calculated from the N for each specific item.

Institutional Type

We disaggregated the findings by institutional type to determine if a difference existed between the types of programs offered in each section. While private schools were more likely to offer a sophomore initiative than were public schools ($\chi^2 = 5.41$, $p = .019$, 1df, $N = 371$), the types of sophomore initiatives offered by responding institutions varied little between schools of different sizes or sources of institutional control. In fact, only two statistically significant differences were found between the offerings of public and private schools; only one such significant difference was found between small (i.e., less than or equal to 5,000 fall 2005 FTE enrollment) and large schools (i.e., greater than 5,000 fall 2005 FTE enrollment). Student government initiatives for sophomores were most common in small ($\chi^2 = 5.02$, $p = .025$, 1df, $N = 110$) and private schools ($\chi^2 = 8.49$, $p = .004$, 1df, $N = 115$), while class events were most frequently used in private schools ($\chi^2 = 9.79$, $p = .002$, 1df, $N = 111$). It is important to note that most private schools in our study are also small (see Tables 2 and 3).

Because students at private schools are more likely to be retained into their second year (ACT, 2006) and progress toward a bachelor's degree on the traditional four-year path (Knapp, Kelly-Reid, & Whitmore, 2006), these schools may be able to more precisely identify a cohort of sophomores. The identification of a sophomore class is a critical component of any sophomore-specific initiative, especially sophomore-class events or representative governing councils. In the remainder of the chapter, we explore in greater depth the specific and intentional initiatives developed for sophomore students.

Table 2
Sophomore Initiatives by Institution Type

Sophomore-Specific Initiatives ($N = 371$)	Public ($n = 153$)	Private ($n = 218$)
Frequency	41	84
Percentage	26.8%	38.5%

$p < .05$

Sophomore Class Events ($N = 111$)	Public ($n = 35$)	Private ($n = 76$)
Frequency	10	46
Percentage	28.6%	60.5%

$p < .01$

Sophomore Student Government Initiatives ($N = 115$)	Public ($n = 38$)	Private ($n = 77$)
Frequency	8	38
Percentage	21.1%	49.4%

$p < .01$

Table 3
Sophomore Initiatives by Institution Size ($N = 110$)

Sophomore Student Government Initiatives	Small ($n = 74$)	Larger ($n = 36$)
Frequency	35	9
Percentage	47.3%	25.0%

$p < .05$

Advising

Academic advising is often a vehicle through which an institution can address curricular and career-related decisions with its students. In fact, an analysis of response patterns indicates that responding schools frequently offer initiatives related to career planning, selection of a major, and academic advising concurrently (see Table 4). The connection between career choice and major selection is evident from the narrative responses as well. A few institutions (e.g., Roberts Wesleyan College) connect these through the advising process, where the advisor is someone coming from career services.

While most sophomore advisors were connected to departments or University Colleges (for undecided students), responses revealed a variety of advising models for sophomores. A few respondents stated that advisors lived in the residence halls. At Emory University, for example, the academic advisor lives in a sophomore residence hall. At SUNY Binghamton peer advisors, called Discovery Assistants, live in the halls and assist with academic advising.

In some instances, students keep their first-year advisor into their sophomore year. This advisor may be a faculty member (e.g., Barnard College, Bates College) or a staff member (e.g., LaSierra University, Beloit College). At Jackson State University, sophomores are assigned both a staff advisor and a faculty advisor to help students pursue their academic and career paths simultaneously, but with different guides.

Whether advisors are students, faculty, or staff, their duties are similar. They assist sophomores as they choose courses and explore majors. They also recommend and arrange for tutoring or other supports, if necessary.

Curricular Offerings

Approximately 20% of the respondents mentioned involvement in some sophomore-specific curricular effort, from offering a credit-bearing course (21.1%) to providing a learning community for sophomore students (17%). The course is often tied to the mission of an institution (specifically) or the ideals of liberal education (more generally). For instance, the course at St. Anselm College, Portraits of Human Greatness, is part of the core curriculum and an interdisciplinary humanities program. At Crown College the course, Spiritual Formation and Leadership, is designed to prepare "students to grow spiritually and in their leadership skills." Developing leadership skills is also the goal of the course at Austin College. At Emory, the course deals with health and wellness issues. DePaul's course is on multiculturalism and is a core curriculum requirement. At Rhodes College, students take a four-course sequence: two in their first year and two in their second. As is the case at Rhodes College, sophomore-specific courses can be part of a larger curricular sequence that transcends traditional class distinctions.

Reflecting an awareness of the unique issues facing sophomores, some courses are tied to major exploration and career planning (e.g., SUNY Binghamton). One such course exists at Emmanuel College in Boston; the college sponsors a noncredit, but required Pre-internship and Career Planning Course for second-year students. Similarly, a half-credit course required for graduation at Susquehanna University focuses on the career decision-making process.

Sophomore-specific courses are not always formal or required. One survey participant explained the content of these programs as "relating career awareness to the major, starting a portfolio, and exploring graduate school options." At Lehigh University, the Career Services Office offers optional programs specifically designed for students throughout their college experience. The programs for second-year students focus on developing internship plans.

Internships were noted as playing a key role in the sophomore year at a number of institutions. These programs tended to be optional for second-year students. At Indiana University Southeast, internships are optional for sophomores but can be credit-bearing or noncredit, paid or unpaid. Some institutions introduce students to the idea of internships in a course. Oglethorpe University, for example, offers a Sophomore Choices course taught by career center staff. The course helps students learn about internships, majors, and graduate schools.

Curricular learning communities, i.e., linking courses and having students take the courses as a cohort, has been helpful in integrating first-year students socially and academically on many campuses (Henscheid, 2004). Narrative responses in this survey suggest that curricular learning communities may also be appropriate for second-year students. Emory University has already initiated such efforts while other campuses mentioned planning to do this in the future (e.g., Loyola College).

Mentoring

On some campuses mentoring plays an intentional role in the second-year experience. In most cases, sophomore students serve as peer mentors for other students (46%); peer mentoring for sophomore students was reported much less frequently (15%). Having just completed their first year successfully, sophomore students are likely well positioned to provide guidance to incoming students. While such an initiative provides direct benefits to the mentored first-year students, it may also provide indirect benefits to the second-year students doing the mentoring. Mentors may improve self-confidence, time-management, and other beneficial skills by helping their mentees (Boice-Pardee, 2005).

In most cases, sophomores serve as mentors to first-year students at orientation, in a first-year seminar, or in the residence halls. However, in some of the cases mentioned, sophomores are not the only student group serving in these capacities. Juniors and seniors may also participate in these ways. Therefore, though second-year students often act as peer mentors for first-year students, these opportunities are not exclusively reserved for sophomores according to the narratives provided by the responding institutions.

Regardless, the benefits of being a peer mentor accrue only to those who actually become peer mentors—usually a limited number of already high-performing students. To reach the mass population of second-year students, some institutions have begun initiatives in which sophomores are the *mentees*. That such initiatives exist is to be expected; perhaps more interesting is the manner in which these mentoring services are provided. A disproportionate number of responding institutions used faculty or staff (31.4%) to mentor their second-year students, while only 15.4% used upper-class students in that role. Perhaps the more frequent use of faculty/staff mentors speaks to the unique challenge of mentoring sophomore students.

Residence Life

Sophomore-specific residence halls were mentioned by approximately one third of the respondents (33.6%). Some institutions mentioned sophomore buildings (e.g., Emory University, University of Denver), and others noted that they have sophomore-designated floors (Macalester College). Sometimes the on-campus accommodations are optional for second-year students (e.g., University of Scranton offers an optional living and learning community). However, many institutions now require second-year students to live on campus (e.g., Lehigh University).

Other institutions offered sophomore-specific programming in their traditional residence halls. Brandeis University provides newsletters and programs for their residential sophomore students. Creighton University offers a "communal, co-ed, service-learning program for selected sophomores based on four distinct [institutional] values: Community, Service, Faith, and Justice." This program is offered to only 56 sophomore students. While many institutions target sub-groups of second-year students, a few institutions talked about training their staff to specifically handle issues that may affect all sophomore students (i.e., Macalester College, University of South Carolina). In addition to specific training, linkages between residence life and sophomore initiatives are sometimes facilitated by leaders holding dual titles. For instance, at St. Michael's College, the coordinator of sophomore development is also the assistant director of residence life. Similarly, the director of sophomore advising at Yale University is also the residential college dean.

Financial Aid

Financial aid is closely tied to students' ability to persist (see Nora, Barlow, & Crisp, 2006, for a review). However, while many of the responding institutions help sophomores find external funding (much like they do for all students), very few of them reported having financial aid specifically earmarked for sophomore students. Two institutions that do offer special funding packages for sophomores are Benedict College and The College of New Jersey. Benedict College mentioned that they offer a $2,500 award to every sophomore earning a minimum of 3.5 cumulative GPA at the end of the first year, and The College of New Jersey has a scholarship program open only to sophomores who have "shown an investment in building community within the residential campus."

Two other unique financial programs have been instituted to support second-year students. Beloit College offers Venture Grants, which students apply for in the second semester of their first year "to travel, do research, start a business" during their sophomore year. Colorado College offers a similar program. (For more information about these institutions' second-year programs, see chapters 4 and 5, respectively.)

Events

Nearly half of the institutions reporting sophomore initiatives offered some type of sophomore class event. Many of the events noted by participating institutions are tied to career and major exploration with career and major fairs and workshops being mentioned most frequently. Beloit College holds a Declaration Fair in December when students "meet with faculty from all departments to discuss majors and options." To encourage attendance at the event, food is offered and it is held on a Sunday night when the dining service is closed. Knox College takes advantage of Fall Institute Day when classes are cancelled and offers workshops and meetings regarding selecting majors. Washington and Lee University offers a Choosing Your Major Resource Fair, which offers one-stop shopping with representatives from academic departments, counseling services, and financial aid to help sophomores. West Virginia University offers Sophomore Adventure Reorientation (SOAR), a "one-week spring/summer outdoor adventure trip for sophomores as they focus on determining a major." This trip is part of a three-credit course with follow-up activities in the fall. Yale offers a Sophomore Advising Night hosted by each residential college for its residents. Emmanuel College in Boston has a Sophomore Pinning Ceremony where second-year students declare their major in front of invited guests and department chairs. Such symbolic rituals reinforce the importance of these decisions and officially welcome students into their major course of study.

Several respondents mentioned community service and/or service-learning as a part of the sophomore-year experience. Some schools require sophomores to complete community service hours. Wittenberg University requires students to complete 30 service hours for graduation while Benedict College sophomores must complete 20 hours of service-learning per semester. College officials hope such service initiatives will help students put "their learning into action and hone their leadership skills." Several of the schools mentioned leadership programs when discussing service-learning (e.g., Furman University, Massachusetts Maritime Academy). Other responding institutions mentioned participating in Habitat for Humanity or local charity events (e.g., Sacred Heart University, William Jewell College).

At other schools, sophomore-class events are primarily social in nature. A wide range of events fall under this category. Charleston Southern University, for example, hosts a welcome-back dance for sophomores in the fall term. Bennington College recently started a collaborative project, Sophomores' Out to Dinner in which faculty and Student Life employees invite sophomores to attend a special dinner. Students are placed into groups of 20 and joined by a recent alum, a faculty member, and the associate dean of students. Emory University offers trips, dinners, and dances for second-year students. In addition, a few schools mentioned offering sophomore retreats (e.g., Mount St. Mary's University, Beloit University) while Washington and Lee University offers sophomore class trips.

Sophomore class events were sometimes set up by sophomore-class councils. These class leaders often plan events for their specific class as a part of their duties (e.g., Knox College, Jackson State University, Appalachian Bible College). At New York University, the class council sponsors trips to local museums. At Oglethorpe University, the sophomore class leadership plans events from ice cream socials to baseball games.

Publications

Of the schools that offer some type of sophomore initiative, only 17% offered a publication for sophomores. Such publications ranged from an electronic newsletter or welcome-back letter to a web site or handbook. At Brandeis University, Residential Life publishes a monthly Sophomore-Year Experience newsletter for each of their sophomore residents. John Jay College offers a newsletter for all sophomore students. The College of New Jersey publishes three or four issues of its newsletter, which offers sophomore-specific information, each semester. Some institutions have web sites designed for second-year students (e.g., University of Denver). Other institutions (e.g., University of Puget Sound) send out e-mails to second-year students at different points during the year highlighting events of interest.

Administration of Sophomore Initiatives

Several institutions mentioned having a person dedicated to serving sophomore students. In addition to Saint Michael's and Yale Universities, Sacred Heart University has a Sophomore/Transfer mentor who will "focus on retention and the overall well being of those students." Salve Regina University also has a dedicated sophomore class advisor.

In all, 36 of the 382 institutions provided narratives regarding the administration of the sophomore programs. A wide range of professionals leads these second-year efforts. Sometimes these administrators have additional responsibilities as evidenced by their titles: director of the Office of Orientation and Transition Services (Syracuse University) and the director of student services and retention services (Xavier University). However, in other cases, these professionals are clearly on the front lines in the institution's efforts to help second-year students (e.g., advisor to the sophomore class at Brandeis University and sophomore class dean at Barnard College). In some instances, it is clear that there are two individuals who coordinate all second-year programs. At Beloit College, the chief student affairs officer and a professor in their modern languages department share administration of sophomore initiatives. In most cases, staff have other duties and sophomore programs are just one piece of their responsibilities.

Correlations Between Types of Sophomore Initiatives

To explore the relationship between various types of sophomore initiatives, a series of phi statistics were calculated (see Table 4). The phi statistic measures the strength of association between two dichotomous variables. As applied to this study, a high positive phi score indicates a strong likelihood that an institution with one type of initiative also has another type of initiative. For example, it is likely that a school with a program to assist in the selection of a major also had sophomore-specific academic advising (phi = .434, $p < .001$) and career planning initiatives (phi = .477, $p < .001$). This association makes intuitive sense as academic advisors often address both academic and career plans with their students. In addition, institutions with sophomore-class events were likely to also have sophomore-specific initiatives related to student government (phi = .412, $p < .001$), community service (phi = .323, $p < .001$), cultural enrichment (phi = .306, $p < .01$), and publications (phi = .340, $p < .001$).

The correlations among various initiatives demonstrate the considerable opportunity for institutions to simultaneously address several sophomore-related issues. There are two possible reasons for a high phi score. Either schools had two separate initiatives, or they had an initiative that simultaneously works to address two issues relevant to sophomores. In the case of associations between academic advising, career planning, and selection of a major, the second explanation is likely most accurate. Schools successfully interweaving these three elements are maximizing the number and type of sophomore initiatives while minimizing expenditures of labor and other scarce resources. Such cases may provide a model for cost-effective implementation of sophomore-specific initiatives.

Table 4
Associations Between Sophomore Initiatives

Initiatives Geared Toward Sophomore Students	Academic advising	Career planning	Class events	Community service / service-learning	Credit-bearing course	Cultural enrichment activities	Curricular learning communities
Academic advising	1						
Career planning	.241*	1					
Class events (e.g., trips, dinners, dances)	.151	.275**	1				
Community service / service-learning	.407***	.238*	.323***	1			
Credit-bearing course (e.g., sophomore seminar)	-.044	.017	.033	-.038	1		
Cultural enrichment activities (e.g., plays, musical events, multicultural fairs)	.335***	.161	.306**	.419***	.107	1	
Curricular learning communities (i.e., linked courses)	.196	.031	.060	.255*	.146	.089	1
Faculty/staff mentors for sophomore students	.480***	.173	.240*	.430***	.052	.181	.252*
Financial aid (e.g., sophomore scholarships, loans)	.253*	.154	.022	.434***	.086	.411***	-.114
Opportunities to co-teach or assist in teaching a class	.144	.074	.137	.177	.117	.064	.150
Peer mentors by sophomores (i.e., sophomores mentoring other students)	.228*	.102	.049	.149	.080	.126	.150
Peer mentors for sophomores (i.e., students mentoring sophomores)	.249*	.102	.053	.268**	.148	.217*	.160
Programs to assist in selection of a major	.434***	.477***	.219*	.285**	-.088	.127	.007
Publications for sophomore students (e.g., sophomore newsletter or web site)	.007	.255**	.340***	.180	.066	.050	.004
Residence life (e.g., sophomore-specific living arrangements)	.123	.169	.122	.178	-.016	.124	.213*
Student government (e.g., sophomore council)	-.013	.193*	.412***	.133	.066	.042	-.040
Other	-.063	.177	.210	.178	-.187	.084	-.258

Note. The phi statistic measures the strength of association between two dichotomous variables. As applied to this study, a high positive phi score indicates a strong likelihood that an institution with one type of initiative also has another type of initiative.

**p* < .05
***p* < .01
****p* < .001

Faculty/ staff mentors for sophomore students	Financial aid	Opportunities to co-teach or assist in teaching a class	Peer mentors by sophomores	Peer mentors for sophomores	Programs to assist in selection of a major	Publications for sophomore students	Residence life	Student government	Other
1									
.157	1								
.078	.090	1							
.300**	.097	.234*	1						
.157	.017	.076	.296**	1					
.392***	.259*	.026	.264**	.197*	1				
.304**	002	.047	.082	.056	.208*	1			
.228*	.189	-.080	.000	.155	.115	.200*	1		
.182	.091	.130	.089	.089	.131	.200*	.207*	1	
.080	.241	-.102	-.025	.256*	.125	.401***	.069	.159	1

Assessment of Sophomore Initiatives

Of the responding institutions with sophomore initiatives, only 29.5% have assessed their efforts. When conducted, assessments of sophomore initiatives tended to involve the use of locally developed surveys (58.8%), focus groups (57.1%), and institutional data analysis (54.3%). Some institutions assessed their initiatives using multiple methods. See Table 5 for complete details.

Table 5
Types of Assessment Conducted on Sophomores

Assessment Method	Frequency	Percentage
Locally developed survey (*n* = 34)	20	58.8
Analysis of institutional data (*n* = 35)	20	57.1
Focus groups (*n* = 35)	19	54.3
Individual interviews (*n* = 34)	10	29.4
Commercially available survey (*n* = 33)	5	15.2

Assessment of sophomore initiatives may prove critical to their increased use and success. Proper assessment will allow educators to measure the effectiveness of such initiatives and identify opportunities for their improvement. The proper collection and use of assessment data has been cited as critical to the foundation and advancement of initiatives designed to improve the first year of college; with proper use, it could play a similar role in the advancement of sophomore-year initiatives as well. For example, the sophomore programs at Beloit College, a school that has had sophomore programs for many years, have undergone continuous improvement by purposefully refining their offerings based on feedback from assessment.

However, narrative responses from the survey suggest that, for many schools, sophomore initiatives are relatively new phenomena that have not had sufficient time for formal assessments. The limited implementation of sophomore initiatives to this point allows institutions to build assessment processes into the initiative during the early stages of planning and implementation.

For schools with fledgling sophomore initiatives, simple assessments have the potential to shape future development. To that end, Macalester College conducts brief evaluations after each event. Other schools use surveys to assess their efforts. The University of Puget Sound assesses their mentor program with an e-mailed questionnaire, while Union College in New York surveys students about advising. At Asbury College, each department develops a survey instrument "to determine the effectiveness of the[ir] program or event." Hardin-Simmons University, Johns Hopkins University, and New York University use broad surveys in an attempt to get a more general sense of their sophomore class.

Relatively few schools mentioned that they conducted focus group or interview assessments. Sometimes interviews were used to get clarification of survey data (i.e., Johns Hopkins University), but at Rensselaer Polytechnic Institute sophomores are randomly selected to participate in focus groups with the class dean six times per year. Thus, the assessments serve a range of institutional objectives. Some may have been closely linked to a program (e.g., advising at Union College) while others provide a broader sense of the sophomore experience (e.g., Oregon State).

A number of institutions provided information regarding the findings from their assessments. Those findings are closely linked with the objectives of the research. For instance, Asbury College was interested in finding out if their career services initiatives were helping sophomores become more focused on their majors. The survey findings helped them refine and improve their efforts in this area. Johns Hopkins cast a wider net to get a broader sense of student needs. They found that the students wanted more focus on internship opportunities as opposed to basic major exploration.

They also wanted more information on campus housing options. Finally, the sophomores at Johns Hopkins wanted more support in student leadership positions and more opportunities to serve in leadership development programs as mentors.

A few of the findings seemed particularly interesting and may be ripe for additional study. Lewis and Clark College discovered that sophomores who studied abroad were less likely to be retained than students who took advantage of this opportunity in their junior year. Trinity University students stated that it was harder to try new things in the sophomore year than in their first year. Students felt they were supposed to already be connected by their second year; whereas, in the first year, students contended that it was okay not to know anyone. First-year students apparently feel a sense of freedom associated with starting something new that evaporates as they become more enmeshed in an institution. Generally, institutions that assessed their programs in terms of retention mentioned seeing improvement.

Future Sophomore Initiatives

Just over one third (37.3%) of responding institutions were planning some type of future sophomore initiative (see Table 6). Schools that already had sophomore initiatives were more likely to be planning future sophomore initiatives (65.9%) than schools that do not yet have any sophomore initiatives (35.9%) ($\chi^2 = 22.01$, $p = .000$, 1df, $N = 351$).

Table 6
Developing Future Sophomore Initiatives ($N = 351$)

	Frequency	Percentage
Yes	131	37.3
No	163	46.6
Don't Know	57	16.2

A wide range of efforts are in the planning stages at participating institutions, though many of those initiatives are still in the early stages of discussion at the time of this writing. Plans for future initiatives generally mirror the initiatives already in place: sophomore courses, sophomore residence halls or floors, sophomore-specific advising that helps students concentrate on career and major exploration, welcome events, leadership retreats, class trips, and cultural events. In an effort to ensure effective educational practice, many of the schools mentioned waiting on assessment results before beginning new initiatives, while others stated that conducting assessments was their future initiative.

Conclusion

Results presented in this chapter offer a glimpse into the current state of sophomore-year initiatives at the participating institutions. These findings paint a national picture, allowing readers to consider the detailed program descriptions of later chapters in light of the national perspective. As you consider the initiatives described later in this monograph, it might be helpful to remember three key findings from this study. First, initiatives to improve the sophomore-year experience come in all shapes and sizes. There is no silver bullet, and most schools have adopted highly customized initiatives to address the issues unique to their campuses. Second, it appears that sophomore-specific efforts are just beginning. With more than 130 schools reporting plans for future sophomore initiatives, schools considering them can rest assured they will not be the only institution with programs specifically geared toward their second-year students. Finally, assessment is key to the continued success of second-year initiatives. Several schools have effectively used assessment to improve educational practice, and many are in the midst of doing so. We have much work to do. Retention numbers are the first warning sign that these students need our attention. This exploratory survey suggests that the programs we do offer need to be assessed and that we must devote more time and resources into the development of programs for second-year students. Let this work provide the charge to educators to refocus their efforts to provide needed assistance to this too often invisible population.

References

American College Testing (ACT). (2006). *National collegiate retention and persistence to degree rates.* Iowa City, IA: Author. Retrieved April 19, 2006 from, http://www.act.org/path/policy/pdf/retain_2006.pdf.

Boice-Pardee, H. (2005, March 10). Assessing peer education: What can we learn? Essay for the First-Year Assessment Listserv. Retrieved August 23, 2007 from, http://www.sc.edu/fye/resources/assessment/essays/Boice-Pardee-3.10.05.html.

Burke, J. M. (2005). *2005 higher education directory.* Falls Church, VA: Higher Education Publications.

Henscheid, J. M. (2004). First-year seminars in learning communities: Two reforms intersect. In J. M. Henscheid (Ed.), *Integrating the first-year experience: The role of learning communities in first-year seminars* (Monograph No. 39, pp. 1-8) Columbia, SC: University of South Carolina, National Resource Center for The First Year Experience and Students in Transition.

Knapp, L. G., Kelly-Reid, J. E., & Whitmore, R. W. (2006). *Enrollment in postsecondary institutions, fall 2004; graduation rates, 1998 & 2001 cohorts; and financial statistics, fiscal year 2004.* Washington, DC: U.S. Department of Education. Retrieved April 19, 2007 from http://nces.ed.gov/pubs2006/2006155.pdf

Nora, A., Barlow, L., & Crisp, G. (2006). Examining the tangible and psychosocial benefits of financial aid with student access, engagement, and degree attainment. *American Behavioral Scientist, 49*(12), 1636-1651.

Packard, B.W. (2004-2005). Mentoring and retention in college science: Reflections on the sophomore year. *Journal of College Student Retention: Research, Theory, & Practice, 6*(3), 289-300.

Appendix A

Methodology

The study is based on data gathered from the 2005 National Survey of Sophomore-Year Initiatives. This new instrument asked respondents to indicate whether or not their campus offered any initiatives specifically or intentionally geared toward sophomore students (see Appendix B). Subsequent yes/no/don't know questions allowed respondents to identify the specific types of initiatives offered, while open-ended questions offered respondents the opportunity to describe the objectives and administration of their initiatives. To avoid any confusion, the survey prominently displayed, on every survey page, the study's definition of sophomores: students in their second year of postsecondary education. This definition evolved from two recognitions. First, students tend to identify themselves as sophomores in their second college year, regardless of how many credit hours they bring with them to the institution (e.g., AP credits) or earn during the first year. Second, institutional supports for first-year students tend to expire once a student returns to campus for a second fall term, not when a student (perhaps with AP or similar credit) reaches an arbitrary credit threshold.

The web-based survey instrument was piloted in July 2005. After revising the instrument based on suggestions from the pilot test, official survey administration occurred in October 2005. An e-mail was sent to the chief student affairs officer at all regionally accredited public and private four-year baccalaureate-granting institutions in the 50 US states ($N = 1{,}278$) as identified by the *2005 Higher Education Directory* (Burke). Note that two-year institutions were excluded because the complex mix of students at those institutions makes identification of a "sophomore" year problematic. Survey recipients were asked to forward the e-mail to the administrator best suited to complete the survey. This option enabled the survey to be completed by the institutional representative most familiar with the requested information.

Invitations to participate in the survey were successfully e-mailed to 1,139 institutions (139 of the original 1,278 emails were bounced-back as errors). After two reminders and data clean up, a total of 382 institutions (33.5%) successfully completed the survey.

Researchers ran frequencies to identify the most common types of initiatives in place for second-year students. Additional chi-squared analyses (and Fischer's exact test, when needed to confirm chi-squared test findings) were performed to see if responses varied across institutional control or size. In addition, phi statistics were calculated to explore correlations between various types of initiatives at individual schools. Respondent answers of "don't know" are considered in frequency tabulations but are treated as missing values in the calculation of most chi-squared, phi, and Fisher's exact test statistics. In addition, a qualitative analysis, in which responses patterns were identified, compared, and confirmed by the lead researchers, was performed on the open-ended questions.

The quantitative and large-scale nature of this study required an a priori selection of the initiative types to be included in the survey. We created the list of 17 initiative types drawing on two resources developed by The National Resource Center: (a) posts to the SOPH-List (a 500+ member discussion listserv for educators interested in the second year of college) and (b) descriptions of sophomore initiatives at more than 30 institutions compiled on the Center's web site. Some institutions offered more than one initiative that would fall into the same category (e.g., several initiatives to help students choose a major). At other institutions, the same initiative would fall into multiple categories (e.g., a credit-bearing sophomore course that addressed academic advising issues). Therefore, because neither the campus initiatives nor the survey categories are mutually exclusive, the resulting analysis should not be considered a precise record of individual programs, but rather an initial exploration of current practices related to sophomore students.

The range of sophomore-year initiatives involves both academic (e.g., course offerings and learning communities) and student affairs divisions (e.g., career exploration and class events). Although we hope there is collaboration between the divisions, such collaboration cannot be assured. Distributing the survey through the chief student affairs officers may have affected the response patterns, and consequently, the survey findings may underrepresent academic affairs initiatives.

Finally, while the sample is not fully representative of the nation's colleges and universities (large and public schools are overrepresented, see Table 7) the collection of these data from 382 schools represents the most substantial portrait of sophomore-year initiatives currently available.

Table 7
Survey Respondents by Institutional Type ($N = 351$)

	National Percentage	Survey Responses Percentage
Public Small	10.9	11.5
Public Big	17.9	28.9
Private Small	64.7	53.9
Private Big	6.6	5.6

Note: Small schools are those with a fall 2005 FTE enrollment of 5,000 or fewer; big schools are those with fall 2005 FTE enrollment of greater than 5,000. Five schools did not indicate public or private, while 26 institutions did not indicate their enrollment. These schools are omitted from the analysis. National percent was calculated from NCES/IPEDS data collected April 27, 2006.

Appendix B

2005 National Survey of Sophomore-Year Initiatives

Please select your response to each question by clicking in the appropriate space. When finished answering the questions on a page, please click on the "continue" button at the bottom of that page. The survey should take approximately 15 minutes to complete. Please complete the entire survey in one sitting—there is no way to save the survey and return to it later. Thank you for your participation.

To help us ensure that only one survey is completed for each school, please enter the name of your institution below.

Institution: ______________________________

For the purposes of this survey, we are defining sophomores as students in their second year of post-secondary education.

Does your institution currently offer any initiatives specifically or intentionally geared toward sophomore students?

- ☐ Don't know
- ☐ No
- ☐ Yes

INITIATIVES

In which of the following areas does your institution currently have initiatives specifically or intentionally geared toward sophomore students? (On the next page of the survey you will have the opportunity to describe your institution's initiatives in more detail.)

	Don't know	No	Yes
Academic advising	☐	☐	☐
Career planning	☐	☐	☐
Class events (e.g., trips, dinners, dances)	☐	☐	☐
Community service/service learning	☐	☐	☐
Credit-bearing course (e.g., sophomore seminar)	☐	☐	☐
Cultural enrichment activities (e.g., plays, musical events, multicultural fairs)	☐	☐	☐
Curricular learning communities (i.e., linked courses)	☐	☐	☐
Faculty/staff mentors for sophomore students	☐	☐	☐
Financial aid (e.g., sophomore scholarships, loans)	☐	☐	☐
Opportunities to co-teach or assist in teaching a class	☐	☐	☐
Peer mentors *by* sophomores (i.e., sophomore students mentoring other students)	☐	☐	☐
Peer mentors *for* sophomores (i.e., students mentoring sophomores)	☐	☐	☐
Programs to assist in selection of a major	☐	☐	☐
Publications for sophomore students (e.g., sophomore newsletter or web site)	☐	☐	☐
Residence life (e.g., sophomore-specific living arrangements)	☐	☐	☐
Student government (e.g., sophomore council)	☐	☐	☐
Other (explain on next page)	☐	☐	☐

INITIATIVE DESCRIPTIONS

Please offer more details about the initiatives intentionally or specifically geared toward second-year students. *Be sure to scroll to the bottom of this page to view all questions.*

Career planning

Description of initiative (including objectives, administration, and required/optional)

____

____

____

____

Note. Each "yes" response would generate a request for more information. Above is an example of the survey prompt for participants who indicated they offered career planning initiatives.

ADMINISTRATION

Is there currently an individual in charge of sophomore-year initiatives?

- ☐ Don't know
- ☐ No
- ☐ Yes

What is this person's title? ______________________________

To whom does this person report?

- ☐ Academic affairs
- ☐ Student affairs
- ☐ Both academic and student affairs
- ☐ Other ______________________________

Please describe the sophomore-specific job responsibilities of this person.

____
____
____

Is this position full-time (approximately 40 hours per week)?

- ☐ Don't know
- ☐ No
- ☐ Yes

If less than full-time, does this person have another position on campus?

- ☐ Don't know
- ☐ No
- ☐ Yes, academic affairs administrator
- ☐ Yes, faculty member
- ☐ Yes, student affairs administrator
- ☐ Yes, other position

____
____

ASSESSMENT & PLANNING

Has your institution conducted assessment of your sophomore-year initiatives?

- ☐ Don't know
- ☐ No
- ☐ Yes

If yes, which of the following methods have been used?

	Don't know	No	Yes	If yes, please describe method/instrument
Commercially available survey instrument(s)	☐	☐	☐	
Locally developed survey instrument(s)	☐	☐	☐	

Focus group(s)	☐	☐	☐	
Individual interview(s)	☐	☐	☐	
Analysis of institutional dataset(s)	☐	☐	☐	
Other	☐	☐	☐	

If yes, please describe the findings from your assessment of sophomore-year initiatives.

____

____

____

____

Is your institution creating or developing any future initiatives specifically or intentionally geared toward sophomore students?

☐ Don't know
☐ No
☐ Yes

If yes, please briefly describe the future initiatives.

____

____

____

Is there anything else we should know about the sophomore-year initiatives on your campus?

____

____

____

NEW CONTACT PERSON

Would there be another person on your campus who might be better able to complete the National Survey on Sophomore-Year Initiatives?

☐ No
☐ Yes

If yes, please submit his/her contact information

New Contact's Name: ____________________________

New Contact's Title: ____________________________

New Contact's E-mail: ____________________________

Institution: ____________________________

BACKGROUND

Name of person completing survey: ____________________________

E-mail: ____________________________

Institutional setting:

- ☐ Two-year
- ☐ Four-year

Institutional type:

- ☐ Public
- ☐ Private
- ☐ Proprietary

Institutional size:

Fall 2004 FTE Undergraduate	
☐	5,000 or fewer
☐	5,001 – 10,000
☐	10,001 – 15,000
☐	15,001 – 20,000
☐	more than 20,000

Chapter 3

Examining the Experiences of Second-Year Students at a Private Liberal Arts College

Ann M. Gansemer-Topf, Joyce M. Stern, & Mimi Benjamin

The second year of college is garnering attention on many campuses because it is a time when academic and behavior problems may increase and student persistence declines (Gardner, Pattengale, & Schreiner, 2000). In response, institutions are developing programs and activities focused on this group of students (National Resource Center, n.d.). Despite this increased institutional focus, little research has been conducted that examines this population of students. As Gardner et al., state, "While the sophomore slump has been satisfactorily identified, there are insufficient data and research describing the phenomenon. Therefore, we would challenge educational research to pay more attention to this critical transition during the undergraduate experience" (p. 90). The purpose of this qualitative study is to identify the needs and experiences articulated by second-year students at a small, liberal arts college. Our desire is that faculty, staff, and administrators in student and academic affairs can use this information to intentionally create environments that address the specific needs of second-year students.

Theoretical and Conceptual Framework

Although the idea of a "sophomore slump" has existed since the mid-1950s (Freedman, 1956), currently there is a renewed interest in examining this population of students. The critical role of the first-year experience in student persistence has been well documented (Astin, 1993; Tinto, 1993). As a result, colleges and universities developed a variety of programs and initiatives (e.g., learning communities, new student orientation, first-year seminars) designed to engage the first-year student in his/her college environment. Since most of these institutional activities are developed on the premise that the greatest amount of attrition occurs between the first and second year (Tinto), most of these initiatives no longer continue once a student becomes a sophomore. However, Flanagan (1991) found that at selective liberal arts colleges, second- to third-year attrition was higher than first- to second-year attrition.

Researchers who have studied the second-year experience (Anderson & Schreiner, 2000; Gardner, 2000; Pattengale, 2000) have noted that the second year poses unique challenges. They are "no longer naïve about the college experience, but they may not be fully engaged in it" (Gardner et al., p. 90). In chapter 1 of this monograph, Molly Schaller provides information for understanding these challenges as they relate to the development of college sophomores. In addition to these developmental factors, the institutional environment also can influence the second-year experience.

Institutional Factors

As second-year students experience a new set of developmental challenges, institutions often lack the time and resources to dedicate to this group of students. Unlike the beginning of college when many institutions develop programs that specifically are created with first-year student needs in mind, very few institutions continue these focused efforts into the second year: "Campuses generally allow sophomores to be served by 'normal' processes, not by any special efforts to continue their engagement in learning" (Evenbeck, Boston, DuVivier, & Hallberg, 2000, p. 80). At a time when the academic curriculum intensifies and students are feeling more pressure to solidify an academic plan of study, there is a greater need for academic advising that addresses these concerns (Kramer, 2000). Yet advising services may not adapt to meet these changing needs: "Students need assistance but find little outreach" (Kramer, p. 99).

Many residence hall policies also contribute to a second-year student's lack of involvement or commitment. Because on many campuses second-year students are dispersed throughout on-campus housing (Pattengale, 2000), seeking interpersonal relationships and support among their peers can be challenging. In other instances, students who have not developed friendships by the second year may feel even more isolated and unsure of their ability to establish new relationships than first-year students (Schaller, 2005).

Purpose of the Study

The goal of our study was to explore the experiences and needs of second-year students to better understand their lived experiences. Schaller (2005) completed a qualitative study conducting individual interviews and focus groups with 19 second-year students. Our study built upon this work by interviewing a greater number of students and by including both second- and third-year students. By interviewing students who are in the midst of their second year as well as third-year students who can reflect back on their experiences, we sought to gain insight into the unique aspects of the second year and to identify the factors that may positively or negatively impact the second-year experience.

Past studies have been conducted at mid-sized and large institutions (Juillerat, 2000; Schaller, 2005); whereas, this study was conducted at a small, highly selective, residential liberal arts college. Data that result from interviewing a greater number of students in a smaller environment that stresses a liberal arts education over a career-focused degree can provide insight into the potentially unique experiences of second-year students in select settings. Our hope is that the results can provide institutional leaders with information about this population of students and ideas on how to enrich the second-year experience.

Methodology

A phenomenological approach serves as the methodological framework for this study. Phenomenology is defined as "the study of lived experiences and the ways we understand those experiences to develop a worldview. It rests on an assumption that there is a structure and essence to shared experiences that can be narrated" (Marshall & Rossman, 1999, p. 112). Phenomenological research describes both people's experience and their thoughts about their experience of the phenomenon studied (Glesne, 1999). The phenomenon in this case is the experience of the sophomore year at a specific liberal arts institution, which is common to all of the participants.

Research Site

This study was conducted at a small, residential, highly selective college in the Midwest. Students enter the college without declaring a major. Before arriving, they sign up for a first-year seminar course for the fall semester. The instructor of this course serves as their advisor until the students declare their major. First-year seminars are interdisciplinary and uncorrelated with a specific department or prospective major. Most students delay the major declaration process until the end of the sophomore year, because they are not required to declare a major until preregistration for the fifth semester. A four-year, academic course plan, consisting of all courses that a student plans to take, including all the courses required in the major, is created in consultation with the student's academic advisor. This plan is required of all students as part of the major declaration process. As a residential campus, students have an on-campus residency requirement for all four years. Housing is assigned through a lottery system, preferencing students by class year. Rooms for first-year students are held out of the process, thus students in the second year draw into the lottery last, frequently securing the least coveted rooms.

Participants

Participants in our study were drawn from the population of students who were enrolled in their second and third years at the college; students who transferred into the college from another institution were not included in this study. Comprehensive selection strategies (LeCompte & Preissle, 1993) were used, as all second- and third-year nontransfer students were sent an e-mail inviting them to participate in a focus group. Fifty-four second-year students and 55 third-year students participated in the study, representing approximately 17% of the second-year student population and 18% of the third-year student population. Table 1 illustrates the demographic characteristics of the student population and the sophomores and the juniors who participated in the study.

Table 1
Characteristics of All Students, Second-Year, and Third-Year Students

	Percentage of All Students	Percentage of Second-Year Students (*n* = 55)	Percentage of Third-Year Students (*n* – 54)
Gender			
Male	45.3	25.9	41.2
Female	54.7	74.1	58.2
Ethnicity – Domestic Students			
White/Caucasian	67.0	79.6	70.9
African American/Black	4.2	1.9	7.3
American Indian/Alaska Native	.4	1.9	1.8
Asian American/Asian	5.6	1.9	7.3
Hispanic	4.4	0.0	1.8
Unknown	7.9	7.4	1.8
International Students	10.4	7.4	7.3

Data Collection and Analysis

Focus groups were used as the method of data collection and were particularly fitting for this study because "[t]his method assumes that an individual's attitudes and beliefs do not form in a vacuum: People often need to listen to others' opinions and understandings in order to form their own" (Marshall & Rossman, 1999, p. 114). Data were collected from 11 focus groups with third-year students in fall 2005 and from 10 focus groups with second-year students in spring 2006. The focus groups used a non-standardized interview technique (Denzin, 1978): There was a list of prescribed questions that allowed for follow-up questions by the interviewer. Focus groups were audio-taped and transcribed.

We used inductive coding procedures (Seidman, 1998), reviewing each transcript separately and coding data into specific categories. We then discussed the categories, modified categories as needed, and developed broader themes based on the categories. Themes from each of the focus groups were compared to uncover similarities and differences among participants' responses. Saturation, defined as the point "when the groups become repetitive" (Morgan, 1998, p. 78), occurred as respondents in these groups provided much redundant information. Lastly, we used member checking by allowing participants to review our analysis and provide feedback (Merriam, 1998).

Various approaches were used to ensure trustworthiness. In qualitative research, trustworthiness refers to having results that are credible, transferable, dependable, and confirmable (Guba & Lincoln, 1998). Trustworthiness was ensured through triangulation of data, member checking, and peer debriefing (Guba & Lincoln). Triangulation involves using multiple investigators or multiple sources of data to arrive at findings (Merriam, 1998). To triangulate the data, two investigators collected and analyzed the data, and we interviewed second- and third-year students from a variety of backgrounds and interests. Member checks involve "soliciting feedback about one's data and conclusions from the people you were studying..." (Maxwell, 1996, p. 94). Results of the data and the conclusions were e-mailed to participants for their clarification or confirmation; three participants responded, with one participant offering further clarification. A peer debriefer was identified and reviewed the results and discussion (Lincoln & Guba, 1985). Finally, thick, rich description was used to address the transferability of the study (Lincoln & Guba) Thick, rich description involves providing great detail about the participants, setting, and themes. The following section outlines the themes that emerged from our data.

Findings

> [W]hen you're in a class where there's people from all years, there's like, a little bit of babysitting for the first-years [by the faculty], like, 'awww I'll help you out,' and then, the juniors are like—they get more attention because they're going to do the research in the summer . . . . or seniors too, like, 'oh I've done all of these things.' And you're like, stuck in the middle, like the middle kid. You're not a first-year, so you're . . . expected to . . . know what's going on . . . .and you don't have the experience that juniors and seniors have . . . .What is our place? We don't really have one. —*Second-year student*

Overall, students articulated that their second year is markedly different than their first year. Students characterized the first year as a year of "excitement" comparing it to "camp," "experimenting," and "fun." The second year was when "reality set in . . ." and as one second-year student stated,

> One of the things I just realized about the second year is that you kind of realize what little time you have left. And it's something you don't realize your first year, and your second year, I feel there's more of a . . . sense of purpose . . . .

Another junior summarized, " . . . it's hard because after your first year the sort of starry-eyed idealism kind of dwindles off and you see things for what they actually are. And sometimes it's just hard to adjust to." Students described a seriousness of purpose to their college experience that wasn't there before.

In describing their experiences, students primarily focused on three different, but interrelated aspects of their lives: (a) academic life, (b) social relationships, and (c) extracurricular activities. The following section will describe these aspects in more detail and highlight other emerging themes.

Academics

Participants discussed their academic experiences by identifying processes, realizations, and their related stressors. Most students experienced the sophomore year as more academically difficult than the first year which, in turn, may cause them to question their academic ability: ". . . [Y]ou start getting really hard courses and then you are not performing as well as in your introductory courses and you start to realize, 'Am I really fit for this major? Am I really stupid?'" Another student described it this way:

> I know like, for me, as far as participating in classes, I had so much more confidence last year. And then last semester I was just like, scared, almost, to talk in my classes. You're taking some of these upper-level classes and it's not just all first-years any more. It's a lot of juniors and seniors as well, and you don't wanna appear like a moron if you don't get something right away.

Important processes in the second year included working with their academic advisor, declaring a major, and creating a four-year academic plan. Finally, realizations about themselves as well as the institutional structure became apparent.

Working with academic advisors. As mentioned earlier, in their first year, the students' first-year seminar instructor serves as their academic advisor. In the second year, students typically find a new advisor, a faculty member in the department in which they want to declare their major. A number of students indicated that they selected an advisor by identifying the professor they liked best. Others used such approaches as asking juniors who lived on their residence hall floors or e-mailing seniors for recommendations. One second-year student said, "I was told by a junior, 'Don't ask somebody to be your advisor that you've never met before.'" One second-year student shared some thoughts on the process:

> I think a lot of it is what you want out of your advisor. But there are some people who know what they want to do . . . and basically need someone to sign a piece of paper for them. Then there are people who really want someone to advise them, even to the point of helping with grad school, and "What should I do with my life" kind of questions.

The student went on to mention an additional issue: Is the faculty member available? "And ... it can get complicated finding an advisor, if you're looking for someone specific, because you really have no way of knowing [if they are staying or leaving the school]." Another second-year student recommended alerting students that professors leave, whether permanently or for sabbaticals.

Some students encouraged selecting an advisor in the student's preferred area of study, while others did not see that as critical. Within the major a student may have specific goals, or they may have goals for life after college related to a particular sub-field within the major. For example, a student bound for veterinary school who plans to major in biology may wonder whether or not it will be advantageous to have an advisor who is a microbiologist rather than a plant biologist. One second-year student commented, "I feel like the emphasis, that you know, you have to have someone in your related field, I feel like that can be overrated sometimes, although I probably did luck out."

Declaring a major. Students enter the institution without declaring a major. Officially selecting a major typically occurs after the first year, and discussion around this selection process escalates in the sophomore year. One sophomore student commented, ". . . [T]here's quite a good deal of discussion among people generally . . . about what exactly they want to do with their lives. I think it's probably something to do with the whole having to declare a major." A junior shared that she felt unprepared for the pressure to select a major, stating,

> I think there's . . . [an] emphasis on taking intro classes your first year, and that kind of tripped me up when it came to my second year because my first year I hadn't thought about what I'm gonna major in. I was like, I'm gonna take all these interesting classes, and then second year I came in [and] they're like, "When are you going to declare your major?" Well, I've taken all these classes and they're all intro. I have no idea how this is going to play out, but I have to pick one now.

A number of students spoke about the need to declare a major in order to participate in off-campus study. There seemed to be a desire to study abroad during the junior year, which requires a completed application—including a declared major—by February of the sophomore year. According to one sophomore,

> I know a lot of people who declared a major because they wanted to study off campus, but they didn't really know if this was the major they were gonna stick with, and the profs all say, 'Oh, you can always change later.

Some students spoke about declaring a major as if it was a permanent decision:

> It definitely felt like, you're 20, you're a sophomore, you have to declare your major. I definitely felt like I had to figure out the next 10 years. Because, if you didn't pick the right classes and you weren't going to get the right internship because you didn't have the right experiences, you didn't have the relevant courses for the resume.

However, one junior realized that greater flexibility did exist:

> You don't have to feel locked in by your major. 'Cause I'm like, "Oh I'm an anthro major," . . . [it] doesn't define your future. . . . You don't just have to [think], "I have this one major and now I'm locked into it for the rest of my life."

Perhaps hindsight and greater experience led these juniors to see the flexibility within the situation of declaring a major.

Creating a four-year plan. Students at this institution are required to complete a four-year plan with their academic advisors, as previously described. The four-year plan was discussed a great deal in the focus groups, with some students finding it helpful and others labeling it as problematic and limiting. One second-year student who found the process valuable stated, "I really liked the four-year plan. I felt like it really made me think about what I want to take and how I'm going to do that. And it may not work out, but I've talked to the profs about it, and kinda figured out a good combination of classes." Another second-year student pointed out that the plan "forces you to think ahead." A junior said:

> [The four-year plan] helped me out a whole ton… even in my first year I know how to build a major and get all my distributions. . . . And so that helped me a lot, just to know what I'd have to do in four years. . . .

Students who found the process helpful seemed to recognize its purpose for planning and preparing while also acknowledging that it was a fluid document. One second-year student explained,

> I can understand why they want us to do a four-year plan because, I mean, it is helpful to try to figure out when you're going to fit things in, but I don't know a single person who's ever stuck to their four-year plan. It's impossible. I mean . . . my four-year plan changed two days after I turned mine in.

Those who found the plan frustrating seemed to view it as a document that was not fluid and perhaps committed them in ways they did not want to be committed. The primary complaint about the plan was that students cannot be certain about future course availability. "You don't know what classes are going to be offered, so you *can't* make a four-year plan," claimed one second-year student. However, this same student said "I don't expect to follow my plan," suggesting a recognition that it was fluid but also acknowledging frustration with the inability to finalize the plan.

Students' varied interests also seemed to impact their ability to create a four-year plan and created a realization of the opportunity cost associated with the plan. One student shared:

> As far as my four-year plan, I don't have much confidence or faith in it. Because every semester, the classes change and there're always special topics that I'm really interested in, and I know that I'm going to be abroad one of the semesters next year, so that'll affect which classes I take. If anything it just made me realize that there are classes I can't take.

Students who voiced frustration with creating a plan focused primarily on their inability to create a structure when there were many unknowns, and they perceived the structure as limiting their future academic options.

Curriculum. Students spoke about what they came to understand as the institution's structure and expectations of them. Comments about the curriculum suggested realizations for students about the institution. Many students commented on being encouraged to explore different academic programs and options in the first year while then feeling pressured to select a major, with its attendant requirements, in the second year. Some of these students shared frustrations with what they seemed to feel was a shift from the first to the second year: "I think the whole liberal arts thing, or open curriculum, is kind of a joke. Like, that's the rhetoric. But then you get here and you realize that to complete a major there are all these different requirements." Students' comments suggest that they were not aware or had not given thought to the structure that would result after the first year. Many commented on taking a variety of introductory courses during the first year and not recognizing a need to focus on a particular area of study. Students also began to recognize time limits that impacted choices they would make. One second-year male said,

> For me, decisions just got a lot harder to make because the first two semesters I could take [any] intro I wanted to take. . . . But now it hit me that, "Ok, you've got six semesters left; that's not that long."

Having to make decisions and intentionally plan in the second year seemed to cause some anxiety for the students.

In the second year, students needed to declare their major, choose an academic advisor, and develop their four-year plan. Students began to realize how little time they had to accomplish their goals and that their choices had implications for their future opportunities. These decisions came at a time when students became less sure about their future plans or interests. As one second-year student mentioned: "I think part of the thing I've found this year is that . . . if I want to be able to do anything with my life after I'm out of here that I need to start focusing now, but at the same time I'm less and less sure of what I actually want to be focusing on."

Social Relationships

Social interactions with peers are important for all students but played an especially important role in the second year. Students in our focus groups keenly described their social environment, discussing "friends," people they "hang out" with, and intimate relationships. Students' social landscape shifted from first to second year in a variety of ways. For some students, friendships solidified, other students mentioned a change in their social relationships, and yet other students struggled to find a network of supportive peers.

Solidifying friendships. Some students noted a greater sense of security, beginning the second year with friendships already established. A third-year student noted that "[Second year] was less traumatic because you don't have that added stress of making friends." For many students, the second year was a more rich social experience. They found their existing friendships became more stable. A female second-year student said, "I feel that my friendships were cemented enough that no matter where they live I'll have pretty much the same friends." For others, those relationships deepened. A third-year student reflected, "The number of people I interacted with socially decreased very much sophomore year, but the *quality* increased."

Developing new relationships. Similar to Schaller's (2005) participants, these students mentioned that the second year was a time when new relationships developed. Some students felt more at ease meeting new people in their second year. A female sophomore said, "I think that I am a lot more comfortable talking to people . . . . I feel a lot more comfortable socially this year than last year." Another student echoed, "…[L]ike first year, I was really secluded to the people on my floor and then I started to go out on weekends and started to introduce myself to people—I was comfortable enough to put myself out there." Many of the students commenting about this increased comfort level mentioned this in conjunction with having "public" jobs, such as working as a barista at the student coffee shop or as a cashier at the campus bookstore, thus knowing more faces and having a public persona may make connecting with new people easier.

Other students found that establishing friendships in the second year was very difficult in contrast to the first year. Students shared two reasons for this phenomenon. One group of students noted a lack of opportunities to meet new people. A second-year student commented,

> Something I've noticed [about] the second year is that it's really hard to make new friends—that the first year basically determines your group of friends. . . . It's a small enough school that there's really not a lot of new opportunities to meet new people.

Forming friendships in the first year may be a kind of survival mechanism. As one third-year student said, "It's like we all needed a family [when we came to college]." Yet, the friendships formed out of necessity in the first year may impede forming new relationships in the sophomore year. One second-year student described a perceived isolation to the social environment in the second year:

> I think to a certain extent it's more difficult to make friends your sophomore year because you talk about the tight bonds that people make in the first couple of weeks, and a lot of people, it seems like they just get into comfort zones with the same people. . . . If you don't make friends right away, you're kind of up a creek; because most people, they've got this set, one group of people that they do everything with.

Friendships of choice vs. friendships of convenience. Students described a realization that many "friends" from their first year were established simply out of convenience or circumstance. Many students mentioned that friendships formed around residence hall floors. A third-year student commented, "My first year there were like six girls around us, and we all became pretty good friends, and so my social life was basically centered around that." In the second year, due to a housing lottery system, friendship groups are dispersed throughout campus, requiring students to make efforts to maintain these relationships. When friends are spread out across even a small campus, students are forced to invest more time maintaining and further developing existing relationships. A third-year student reflected, "Yeah, it's harder [on friendships]. I know [my friends are] only a block away, but it's a long way to go." Because of this distance, these friendships from the first year faded, causing students to question the strength of the relationship:

> Last year I had, I felt like I had a ton of friends. We were all really tight, and you know, socially—but now we live on different parts of campus, and that was really hard adjusting to. That part of the social life, like maybe they were friends by convenience? I thought maybe we were closer. . . .

Students commented that in the second year, they needed to become more intentional about their friendships. Since many of their friends lived on different parts of the campus and they found themselves busy with academics, they felt like they needed to make an effort to maintain relationships:

> I think it's definitely hard to find time to make and maintain friends. Even like my best friend complains all the time that I never come visit him. . . . It's hard for me just to get out of my room, to get out of the books, take 10 minutes, walk across campus, say hello. It seems like such a big effort all of a sudden.

For the first time, students were allowed to have choice in roommates, and this had varying results. One female summarized the positive aspects of choosing living arrangements: ". . .[A]nd you can choose who you live with, which helps so much . . . because at least then you have somewhat more of a say in the home situation environment." Other students mentioned that making choices came with new responsibilities. A third-year female student talked about living with friends:

> My first year I was really distant from my roommate. We didn't know each other. We got along, but we didn't really hang out, and that worked. Second year [I was with] all these people that I'd been good friends with first year . . . and that totally rocked our friendship, because it was suddenly a new dynamic where their everyday problems are always in your face.

Another junior reflected:

> First year is difficult because you don't get to choose, for example, your roommate. But in sophomore year, you did choose your roommate, so if there are issues, you feel a lot more guilty, or it kind of strikes closer to home. It's more personal.

Whereas during the first year, friendships may form out of the convenience of residence hall living; in the second year, friendships developed with other students who shared common interests based on academic disciplines or extracurricular activities (e.g., athletic teams, theater or music groups, community service). One female second-year student said, "Almost all of my friends are people that I know through extracurriculars or through classes." Another female second-year student said, "Your social group becomes the people that are inside your major. . . . Not just people you're in class with, but whatever your major is, especially science majors because we have like our area in the building."

Social relationships compete with other priorities. Students frequently reported that their social lives began to take a back seat to other priorities. They found it difficult to maintain friendships due to competing demands on their time including the academic workload, a job, and extracurricular activities. This finding may contradict ideas currently in the literature. In his study, Gardner (2000) found that students drifted away from academics and focused more on peer relationships. In contrast, at this college, students expressed considerable frustration about maintaining social relationships with the increased academic demands and responsibilities of extracurricular and leadership activities. One second-year female student summarized this idea:

> I think that my social life has been very influenced by my academics. I have so much more work and I have also two jobs. . . so, I don't have as much free time as I used to have my first year. So, I've definitely lost a lot of my friends who are like, "Why are you never with us?"

Another second-year female reiterated this point:

> I expected to work hard [in my second year], but I didn't expect to totally sacrifice my social life, which is pretty much what happened. My friends know that there are certain times that I'm in the library or the [student center] and can come by and say, "Hi" . . . for about five minutes and then we'll say, "Good bye, I'm going back to work, and maybe see you at dinner."

Extracurricular Activities

Second- and third-year students readily described their out-of-class experiences as changing in the second year, whether involvement with a student organization, a campus job, a sports team or music ensemble, or all three. Shifts in the amount or quality of time spent in out-of-class activities varied considerably across the students interviewed. Some reported about the same level of involvement, others increased their involvement finding it easier to join organizations, still others felt the need to cut back due to increased academic demands, and some, perhaps many, focused their time on a few activities and assumed leadership roles.

Most students at this college begin to get involved outside of class during their first year and, for some, their extracurricular activities stayed about the same in the second year. Students reported that becoming involved in extracurricular activities came more easily to them in the second year, and some students found themselves exploring new activities. A junior said,

> I found myself branching out into other extracurriculars that I didn't consider freshman year. I guess I just felt this pressure to kind of investigate [college] a little further and go a little more in-depth in certain things . . . .

Other students see their out-of-class activities as a reflection of how they define themselves. A junior said, "Even the extracurriculars you've chosen are kind of how you define yourself...as opposed to just kind of this big array of confusing choices...your freshman year." This is consistent with the existing literature on developmental changes in the second year; students are wrestling with issues of identity and purpose (Lemons & Richmond, 1987).

For students who persist with the same extracurricular activities, second year allows the opportunity to take on leadership positions. One third-year student reflected back on her experience, "Sophomore year you rise up through the ranks of extracurriculars. You get a lot more responsibility. It turns from you being able to just go to a meeting to *being* the meeting." Many of the leadership positions on this campus are held by second-year students. This may have to do with the nature of the traditional "junior year abroad." A second-year student stated,

> With most juniors going abroad or off-campus to study, you see a lot of organizations, it's the sophomores who take the lead . . . because juniors, traditionally, would be stepping up, but people are away for quite some time . . . .

Similar to their experiences with academics, the second year was also a time when many students realized that they needed to prioritize their activities and make choices. In the past, these students mentioned that they were able to successfully juggle class work, social life, and extracurricular activities. As academic demands increased and extracurricular activities intensified, students found that they "can't do it all." In the second year, many students felt that they had to make choices about the extracurricular activities in which they would participate. A female second-year student said,

> Sometimes I wish I could try out for more of the activities, but ... I have to make choices about what I actually wanna focus on. I like that about this year in that I know what I'm focusing on academically, and so, it's the same way with extracurriculars, too.

Often this meant that they were more intentional, serious and focused about their choices of how to spend their free time: "[I'm doing the] same extracurricular activities, just kind of a difference in, again, with you're expected to be more focused. You know, this is something that you're going to take a lot more seriously than you did your freshman year."

Further, they discovered that they had to say "no" and/or learn effective time management. Many reported needing skills in planning, scheduling, and finding balance. A sophomore said, "I have learned how to schedule my time better this year, so I can balance."

Summary of Major Themes

Although this section was organized to delineate three distinct aspects of the second year, these three areas are not compartmentalized in the student experience. Figure 1 illustrates this interaction. In each of these areas, students are working to develop a sense of purpose. This search for purpose results in students seeking an academic identity in the form of selecting a major, pursuing new relationships, and narrowing their extracurricular activities. All of these take time, and as academic, social, and extracurricular expectations increase, students find themselves continually prioritizing and sacrificing. The realization that they "can't do it all" coupled with a more urgent sense of choosing the "right one" can be a significant source of stress for students.

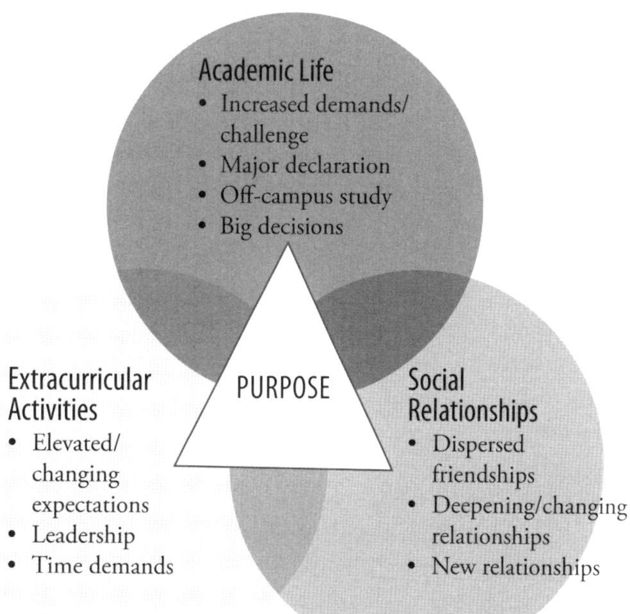

Figure 1. Diagram illustrating the academic, social, and extracurricular challenges for second-year students.

Other Themes

Much of what students discussed has already been documented in previous research. Our study uncovered additional themes not prevalent in the previous literature. For some students, the second year was more stable than their first and third years. Students also talked about the "unexpected" nature of the changes they encountered and the need to work through their difficulties themselves. Lastly, third-year students, with the benefit of hindsight, discussed the value of the struggles of the second year.

Most stable year. Although the majority of students in our study agreed that the second year was difficult, some students welcomed the differences they experienced in the second year. As one junior described: "You are in a safe place. You're not a first-year or an upper-class student. There's a lot more pressure as a junior to start thinking about life after college. Second year is a stable place." For many of these students, the first year was a challenging transition, and they perceived that as upper-class students there would be more pressure to think about life after college. As such, second year provided a safe and stable time in college.

Similar to Schaller's (2005) findings, students who had decided on their academic major and made plans for the future early in their college career or even before entering college did not find the second year especially difficult. One second-year student stated:

> I was gonna say I'm probably actually more focused now than I was—like I'm more sure of what I want to do now than I was in my first year. I mean, to be completely honest, my first semester was pure hell. I mean. . . . and now that I know what I wanna do . . . . It's less indecisive than [the] first year.

Another second-year student echoed this sentiment while acknowledging that her perspective may be different: "I came into [this institution] very focused, and I had no problems my sophomore year. It wasn't too difficult; I was prepared for it . . . . I'm probably the exception."

Unexpected changes and changing expectations. Expectations seemed to change in many areas of their student experience: their academics, social, and extracurricular. Whereas students were prepared to make significant adjustments in their first year, they were surprised that the second year was different than what they had anticipated:

> I expected it to be different [from my first year], but I expected it to be good in a different way, like, . . . and I mean, "sophomore slump" sounds so unbearably cliché, but, something about it just kind of threw me off.

Another student, in describing how she was not prepared for the changes of the second year described it this way: "The first year lasts two years. You get a taste of everything your first year, but nothing really hits you, it's not really real." In discussing her social relationships, a female student in her third year said, "I was surprised that I made new and different friends sophomore year. I expected I would stay friends with those I met first year."

Students also mentioned that faculty seemed to treat them differently. As one student mentioned, "I think that when you become a second year, they [faculty] feel like they don't need to do that [engaging with students] anymore because you've had a year, you can handle it, now you're on your own."

Students spoke of changes in classroom expectations and workload. One student stated, "And I think . . . they just expect that of you a little bit more, to go beyond what they're actually giving you in the classroom, which I think is just . . . it's really a different way of learning . . . ." A second-year student, reflecting on her coursework stated,

> I came back to [school] last semester thinking, "I can do so great." Like, I had this idea that first year had prepared me and that I was a stronger and better writer, and like I knew what [this institution] was all about. . . . [A]nd this is the first time where ALL of my classes are 200-level . . . and I was just plastered with work. I was just sitting there . . . , looking at my calendar, and I was like, "Oh my . . . !"

For those students who have demonstrated commitment to the goals of a student organization and shown dedication in giving their time, there also seemed to be an increased expectation that they would provide continuity for the group and take on more responsibility. One second-year student said, "The further that you get in [extracurricular activities], the more they expect you to do with them, like taking on leadership or organizing things more."

Working on campus while being a full-time student provided similar challenges to students in terms of balancing obligations with their time and, in the second year, taking on increased responsibility. A second-year student said,

> Same is true for on-campus jobs: that after you get through the first year, and, you know, there are a lot of other first-years working, and then once you get to your second year they're like, "You know what you're doing, and we can rely upon you to fill in for people when they're sick . . ." because they know you and [they know you'll work.]

In her quantitative study, Juillerat (2000) concluded that second-year students had higher expectations than other students. In this study, students felt that the institution's (i.e., faculty, staff) expectations of them had changed:

> It seemed to me that most of the changes, the ways in which sophomore year is different from the first year . . . are more, institutional differences, in terms of different mechanisms that second-years have as opposed to first-years, as opposed to "Oh, well, I have a year under my belt, and the experience is different," that it's not a matter of having had more time here, it's a different institution. . . .

Another junior stated,

> I just felt like, sophomore year I was expected to know what I wanted to do, who I was, and kind of, in general, just be comfortable with an understanding of myself and where things were going and how I related with other people . . . .

Others confirmed this expectation that, by the sophomore year, students were expected to exhibit greater independence, maturity of thought, and ability to take care of themselves.

I have to do this myself. After describing their struggles, we asked students if there were any resources that were available to assist them. Students were able to articulate the existing campus services, and many used these services. However, despite knowing about the resources, not all students chose to use them:

> I'm not good at seeking out help when things are bad, and I know there are options . . . . Like, it's not even that I feel weak; I just don't think it would . . . help a lot of the times. And it's like "I don't have the time to waste talking to someone if it's not going to make me feel better . . .

Other students noted that the support that was available did help, but ultimately students felt that they needed to "work it out" on their own:

> I talked to an advisor about my semester last year, but I'm a really analytical person, so I came to her with all of these pros and cons of my behavior and what I could do, and she was a wonderful listener . . . . [T]here was no real action that came out of it, but it was nice to be able to talk to her.

Another student summarized: "It's just you—I mean you still have help and you still have support, ... but it's kind of like, 'All right, now you're on your own' . . . . "

Painful, but beneficial. Juniors who had the opportunity to reflect on their second year were able to recount some of the positive things they learned in their second year. They mentioned that they were able to "set priorities," "manage their time," and "understand their values." One third-year student stated, "I think that the second year was more about learning about who you are, just aside from academics. I know I personally learned a lot about myself just as a person."

Comparing his third year with his second year, one student stated, "That's another difference between sophomore year and this year—you're able to deal with things, you've developed how you deal with situations and so that now you're prepared . . . if something does happen." Another junior described it this way:

> You come [back] after summer, the excitement of the first year is completely gone, everything is kind of blank. Within that because everything's not as special, it's not as new, and I think you're able to look at things more honestly. I was able to develop closer friends, more comfortable in day-to-day life. It's stressful in that expectations are broken down and friendships changed—you have to look at yourself and what you value but it's really good in that once you come out of it you recognize you've changed without very much permanent damage . . . .

Although the second-year was challenging, students who were able to complete their second year learned valuable lessons about themselves.

Conclusions and Implications

Both second- and third-year students were interviewed for this study, and both groups described their second year similarly. Third-year students, with the benefit of hindsight, were able to articulate more of the benefits of the second year than those in the middle of their sophomore year. Students also stated that the second-year forced them to be intentional and more focused. The first year may be described as an all-you-can-eat buffet where students are exposed to all of the options—academic, social, extracurricular—and encouraged to try as many as possible. In the second year, however, students realize that they cannot "have it all" and, therefore, need to plan, prioritize, and focus.

Our results suggest that there may be environmental factors that influence the second-year experience. As such, campus ecology models also may lend insight into the second-year experience. Campus ecology refers to "the mutually shaping interactions between individuals and the environments of a college" (Kuh, Schuh, Whitt, & Associates, 1991, p. 99). As it applies to this study, the campus environment (e.g., the physical spaces, policies, and people) can impact second-year students in a variety of ways. For example, institutional policies may require that students choose a major at the same time that the advisor/student interaction has been de-emphasized structurally (Anderson & Schreiner, 2000). Students are relying more on each other as resources (Gardner, 2000) but find their previous support systems displaced.

The effect of the campus environment is different for second-year students than first-year students. Programs such as new student orientation, learning communities, and first-year seminars are frequently unavailable, but academic, social, and emotional challenges still exist. This begs the question: Is it our sophomores who are slumping or our institutional environments? While we need to be cognizant of the developmental changes occurring in students, we also need to examine how campus environments can lessen or compound the challenges of the second year. Just as new student orientation outlines expectations for first-year students, programs focused specifically on the second year can assist students in similar ways (Batterman, Flanagan, & Ogurtsova, 2003; Gardner, 2000). In their recent article in *About Campus*, Gahagan and Hunter (2006) recommend a list of ways that institutions can enhance the second-year experience. Many of these suggestions (e.g., creating sophomore-appropriate programs, developing second-year traditions) recognize environmental changes that may positively influence and reshape the second-year experience.

The results of this study also suggest that there are students who do not experience these second-year difficulties. Students who see this year as "stable" and are comfortable with the lack of "specialness" may find additional initiatives unnecessary. Other second-year students who are focused and have a sense of direction may benefit from activities such as undergraduate research that are commonly reserved for juniors and seniors. In essence, while this study illustrated that the second year is a unique time for students, not all students experience it in the same way.

Institutions should recognize that the goals of new initiatives should be to support students in their search for meaning and purpose rather than to eliminate this process. Students who were able to successfully manage the challenges of the second year as well as students who struggled found the experiences of the second year beneficial. As one student summarized,

> I don't regret my sophomore year, but it was very difficult; and I think it changes your outlook. What you learn and what is expected of you—but I don't think I would change the fact that it was more challenging, that you need to be more independent. It's a stepping stone, a painful one, but you need to go through it.

References

Anderson, E. & Schreiner, L.A. (2000). Advising for sophomore success. In L. A. Schreiner & J. Pattengale (Eds.), *Visible solutions for invisible students: Helping sophomores succeed* (Monograph No. 31, pp. 55-65). Columbia, SC: University of South Carolina, National Resource Center for The First-Year Experience and Students in Transition.

Astin, A.W. (1993). *What matters in college? Four critical years revisited.* San Francisco: Jossey-Bass.

Batterman, G., Flanagan, W. J., & Ogurtsova, O. (2003). Beloit College sophomore-year program. In M. K. Hemwall & K. C. Trachte (Eds.), *Advising and learning: Academic advising from the perspective of small colleges and universities.* (NACADA Monograph No. 8, pp. 83-90). Manhattan, KS: Kansas State University, National Academic Advising Association.

Denzin, N. K. (1978). *The research act: A theoretical introduction to sociological methods* (2nd ed.). New York: McGraw-Hill.

Evenbeck, S. E., Boston, M., DuVivier, R. S., & Hallberg, K. (2000). Institutional approaches to helping sophomores. In L. A. Schreiner & J. Pattengale (Eds.), *Visible solutions for invisible students: Helping sophomores succeed* (Monograph No. 31, pp. 79-87). Columbia, SC: University of South Carolina, National Resource Center for The First-Year Experience and Students in Transition.

Flanagan, W. (1991). *Sophomore retention: The missing strategy in small college retention efforts.* Unpublished dissertation. University of Wisconsin-Madison.

Freedman, M. B. (1956). The passage through college. *Journal of Social Issues, 12*, 13-27.

Gahagan, J., & Hunter, M. S. (2006, July-August). The second-year experience: Turning attention to the academy's middle child. *About Campus, 11*, 17-22.

Gardner, J. N., Pattengale, J., & Schreiner, L. (2000). The sophomore year: Summary and recommendations. In L. A. Schreiner & J. Pattengale (Eds.), *Visible solutions for invisible students: Helping sophomores succeed* (Monograph No. 31, pp. 89-93). Columbia, SC: University of South Carolina, National Resource Center for The First-Year Experience and Students in Transition.

Gardner, P. D. (2000). From drift to engagement: Finding purpose and making career connections in the sophomore year. In L. A. Schreiner & J. Pattengale (Eds.), *Visible solutions for invisible students: Helping sophomores succeed* (Monograph No. 31, pp. 67-77). Columbia, SC: University of South Carolina, National Resource Center for The First-Year Experience and Students in Transition.

Glesne, C. (1999). *Becoming qualitative researchers: An introduction* (2nd ed.). New York: Longman.

Guba, E. G., & Lincoln, Y. S. (1998). Competing paradigms in qualitative research. In N. K. Denzin & Y. S. Lincoln (Eds.), *The landscape of qualitative research: Theories and issues* (pp. 195-220). Thousand Oaks: Sage.

Juillerat, S. (2000). Assessing the expectations and satisfaction levels of sophomores: How are they unique? In L. A. Schreiner & J. Pattengale (Eds.), *Visible solutions for invisible students: Helping sophomores succeed* (Monograph No. 31, pp. 19-29). Columbia, SC: University of South Carolina, National Resource Center for The First-Year Experience and Students in Transition.

Kramer, G. L. (2000). Advising students at different educational levels. In V. N. Gordon, W. R. Habley, & Associates (Eds.), *Academic advising: A comprehensive handbook* (pp. 84 – 104). San Francisco: Jossey-Bass.

Kuh, G., Schuh, J. H., Whitt, E., & Associates. (1991). *Involving colleges: Successful approaches to fostering student learning and person development outside the classroom.* San Francisco: Jossey-Bass.

LeCompte, M. D., & Preissle, J. (1993). *Ethnography and qualitative design in educational research* (2nd ed.). San Diego: Academic.

Lemons, L. J., & Richmond, D. R. (1987). A developmental perspective of sophomore slump. *NASPA Journal, 24*(3), 15-19.

Lincoln, Y. S., & Guba, E. G. (1985). Establishing trustworthiness. In *Naturalistic inquiry* (pp. 289-331). Newbury Park, CA: Sage.

Marshall, C., & Rossman, G. B. (1999). *Designing qualitative research* (3rd ed.). Thousand Oaks, CA: Sage.

Maxwell, J. (1996). *Qualitative research design: An interactive approach.* Thousand Oaks, CA: Sage.

Merriam, S. B. (1998). *Qualitative research and case study applications in education: Revised and expanded from case study research in education.* San Francisco: Jossey-Bass.

Morgan, D. L. (1998). *The focus group guidebook. Focus group kit 2.* Thousand Oaks, CA: Sage.

National Resource Center for The First-Year Experience and Students in Transition. (n.d.). Sophomore year resources. Retrieved April 18, 2006, from http://www.sc.edu/fye/resources/soph/index.html

Pattengale, J. (2000). Policies and practices to enhance sophomore success. In L. A. Schreiner & J. Pattengale (Eds.), *Visible solutions for invisible students: Helping sophomores succeed* (Monograph No. 31, pp. 31-46). Columbia, SC: University of South Carolina, National Resource Center for The First-Year Experience and Students in Transition.

Schaller, M. A. (2005, July-August). Wandering and wondering: Traversing the uneven terrain of the second college year. *About Campus, 10*, 17-24.

Seidman, I. (1998). *Interviewing as qualitative research: A guide for researchers in education and the social sciences* (2nd ed.). New York: Teachers College Press.

Tinto. V. (1993). *Leaving college: Rethinking the causes and cures of student attrition* (2nd ed.). Chicago: University of Chicago Press.

Authors' Note

We thank Mari Guttman and Cait Scherr for their assistance with the data transcription. We also thank the students of the Class of 2007 and Class of 2008 who volunteered to participate in the focus groups.

Chapter 4

Sophomore-Year Initiative (SYI) Program at Beloit College

William J. Flanagan

Beloit College's Sophomore-Year Initiatives program (SYI) is one of the country's first sophomore-year programs and a pioneer in developing a theoretical approach specifically designed to continue and build upon our First-Year Initiatives Program (FYI), which seeks to integrate students into the academic and social life of the institution. It is our belief that the full integration of students into the life of the college may be, for many, a two-year process.

Beloit's Sophomore-Year Initiatives program officially began in the fall of 1991. SYI was developed as a result of a doctoral thesis research study, which found that most of the 26 small, private colleges surveyed had developed fairly intensive first-year programs for integrating students into their colleges, but virtually no institution continued these efforts during the sophomore year even though many of the institutions surveyed were experiencing significant attrition during the sophomore year (Flanagan, 1991). The goal of this chapter is to describe the research and theoretical rationale for Beloit's SYI program, the institutional context, specific components of the SYI program, and assessment data demonstrating the success of SYI.

Theoretical Basis for Beloit's SYI Program

Many colleges and universities have introduced orientation and first-year programs designed to help students make the transition from secondary to higher education, and these programs have been quite successful (Upcraft, Gardner, & Associates, 1989). Equally important to most institutions is the fact that these initiatives have improved retention primarily because they have, at their core, the goal of promoting student integration with the institution's academic program and social environment. This goal is accomplished through institution-specific programs, policies, and strategies. First-year program planners realize the transition from high school to college can be challenging but also know that students who connect with the institution, both academically and socially, are likely to have a richer, more complete, educational experience—increasing the likelihood they will persist to graduation (Tinto, 1987).

But this critical transition is not accomplished during a weekend, a 10-day program, or even a semester—it is longitudinal and takes time. Nonetheless, many colleges and universities employ a *frontloading strategy*, where an institution reallocates faculty and other institutional resources to better serve students at the beginning of their college experience in order to promote academic and social integration (National Institute of Education, 1984). Noel, Levitz, and Saluri (1986) advocate this approach, suggesting that

> The critical time period in establishing the kind of relationships and one-to-one contacts between students and their teachers and advisors that contribute to student success and satisfaction occur during the first few weeks of the freshman year. It is not uncommon to find that of the students who drop out during the terms of the freshman year (not between terms), 50 percent drop out during the first six weeks (Myers, 1981). If students make it through that high-risk first year and return for the sophomore year, experience indicates the attrition rate begins to drop off by almost 50 percent each succeeding year. (p. 20)

But while this practice of frontloading has produced positive results for many institutions, recent research initiatives have suggested that similar efforts may be worthwhile at the sophomore level. If it is true, as Tinto suggests, that students are likely to persist at institutions where they feel academically and socially integrated into the life of the college, then it seems that efforts to promote student academic and social integration should continue during the sophomore year.

In fact, it can be argued that the most difficult period of the transition process for students may occur during the sophomore year when they may encounter the infamous sophomore slump. Lemons and Richmond (1987) define sophomore slump as a "period of developmental confusion" and, using Chickering's (1969) theory of student development, hypothesize that institutions would do well to recognize that "sophomore slump results from students' struggles with achieving competence, desiring autonomy, establishing identity, and developing purpose" (p. 18). Consequently, institutions may find that devising programs, policies, and strategies focused on the developmental needs of students during this important period will improve the campus climate and retention.

The sophomore year is likely to be the time when students find they cannot obtain the courses, housing, financial aid, or type of academic advising and institutional attention they may have received as first-year students. For sophomores, college is no longer new. The excitement and thrill of a new experience has worn away, and they now face the reality that college will be three more years of hard work, courses, papers, and significant financial investment. These feelings of transition also come at a time when students may be experiencing an "existential crisis," struggling to determine career goals, dealing with personal development issues, and experiencing other diversions that may make academic and social integration even more difficult to attain. For many students, this is the time when they lose their focus and feel alienated from family and friends (Flanagan, 1991).

It may be that students are experiencing what is described as culture shock (Lewis & Jungman, 1986). The culture-shock theory describes a transitional and longitudinal process, similar to Tinto's integration theory, which most people experience as they adapt to a new culture. There are six phases that describe the transition from one culture to another and create, depending on the phase, high, normal, or greatly depressed emotions. In the first stage, called the preliminary phase, which occurs prior to arrival in a new culture, a person experiences a great sense of excitement and anticipation that continues to build through the second, or spectator, phase. As the person becomes more involved with the new culture and feels some of the isolation of being a foreigner, the sojourner gets more depressed throughout the increasing participation phase. During the next period, called the shock phase, the person's emotions bottom out, and

> sojourners have a kind of existential confrontation with the abyss of meaninglessness that separates the two cultures the individual has internalized. Once the effects of facing this abyss have abated, subsequent experience usually leads to a more thorough adaptation to the culture. This phase, the adaptation stage, leads the sojourner to feel identification with the host culture, a feeling of belonging, acceptance, a sense of shared fate. (Lewis & Jungman, p. xxii)

The final, or reentry, phase occurs when the sojourner returns home and feels culture shock in reverse.

This cultural adjustment theory parallels quite closely the stages students go through as they make the separation from home and family, begin the process of adapting to a new environment/culture, and eventually integrate/adapt into the academic and social life of the institution as Tinto describes in his Student Integration Theory (SIG) (1987). While this process may span the entire college experience, many researchers agree that the first two years are the most critical (Noel et al., 1986; Pascarella, Terenzini, & Wolfle, 1986; Terenzini & Wright, 1987). Why, then, would institutions so concerned about retention place all their emphasis on first-year students (and new transfer students) but seemingly ignore sophomores, who are at an extremely vulnerable point in their college careers? Consequently, it would not be surprising if the retention rate between the sophomore and junior years is problematic at institutions where a coordinated and comprehensive approach to retention is not employed during the sophomore year, even if specific and comprehensive efforts had been made in the first year. Students might begin to feel alienated and such feelings might be an indication that students had not completed their integration into the academic and social life of the college which would, in all probability, increase the likelihood of attrition. In short, front-loading may prove to be successful in retaining students during the first college year, but failing to continue appropriate retention efforts during the sophomore year may prove to be a costly mistake for institutions concerned with vital enrollment.

Even when institutions recognize that sophomore students may be facing a difficult period in their personal and academic development, they often do not respond appropriately: They fail to meet student needs in a comprehensive and coordinated way. For example, Noel et al. (1986) describe Tinto's thinking on student departure as reflecting "the unique experience of a particular institutional environment characterized by distinct academic and social communities" (p. 449). Lemons and Richmond (1987) suggest that the institutional academic and social environment might be enhanced if attention were paid to the developmental issues faced by sophomores when attempting to integrate both academically and socially, particularly their "struggle to achieve competence," desire for autonomy, and attempts to establish identity and develop purpose (p. 18). One could infer that students who have achieved this level of development would be more likely to feel integrated into the academic and social life of the college and would more likely be retained. Therefore, it seems that institutions interested in the student-retention issue would begin to design retention strategies, policies, and programs with the specific developmental needs of the sophomore student in mind.

Flanagan (1991) studied 26 small, private, residential, liberal-arts colleges—including Beloit. He found that very few institutions have relevant programs, policies, or strategies in place to help students through the critical second year of college, a period when students the institution would like to retain are quite susceptible to leaving or transferring to another college or university where the "grass may appear greener." Other findings from this study include:

1. Most of these institutions made effective and comprehensive efforts to retain students during the first year but failed to continue those efforts during the sophomore year, when the retention problem is most acute. The sophomore year was the missing strategy in small-college retention efforts.
2. The longitudinal nature of student integration was found to be significant, which supports Tinto's Student Integration Theory (SIG). In addition the survey instrument used for this study focused on six key variables that explain student persistence: (a) academic integration, (b) social integration, (c) skills and ability, (d) ability to pay, (e) significant other's influence, and (f) environment. The study found the persistence variables of academic integration, student skills and ability, and environment were significant for predicting persistence. Ability to pay, significant other's influence, and social integration variables were not found to be as significant in predicting retention.

3. Efforts begun to integrate students into the intellectual and social life of the college during the first year should continue in order to address the developmental needs of students during the sophomore year when they confront the notorious "sophomore slump."
4. The instrument developed for this study called the "Retention Study Model" was found to be effective in measuring institutional retention efforts in both the first and second years.

As a result of its participation in Flanagan's research, Beloit formed a group of faculty, administrators, and students to design a sophomore-year program that would build on the foundation developed during the first-year program (First-Year Initiatives, FYI). The close collaboration of these groups made it possible for the College to implement a program that continues efforts to address the transition from high school to college, academic and social integration, and the unique developmental tasks that sophomore students are likely to face during this crucial year. What follows is a description of Beloit's Sophomore-Year Initiatives Program and the intended and unintended results of the program.

Institutional Context

Beloit College is an independent, residential, national college of the liberal arts and sciences, founded in 1846. Beloit is Wisconsin's first college. A student body of 1,250 is drawn from 49 states and 48 countries resulting in significant geographical and cultural diversity. One in five students is non-Caucasian, and a wide variety of religious orientations and socioeconomic backgrounds are represented on campus. Nearly 94% of the students live on campus, which is located on the border between Wisconsin and Illinois. Beloit College is a member of the Associated Colleges of the Midwest (ACM).

Beloit has a century-old tradition of domestic and international off-campus study opportunities, and more than half of new Beloit graduates will have studied and/or conducted research in such a program. Most of Beloit's students will participate in one or more of the experiential learning opportunities available including internships, field terms, summer employment opportunities, and research activities where students learn by doing. Moreover, the College's curricular foci emphasize experiential, international, and interdisciplinary learning. Findings from Beloit College's participation in the National Survey of Student Engagement (NSSE) demonstrate an institution where students clearly value their opportunities for engaging the in- and out-of-class learning environments. In fact, the College's cocurriculum is specifically designed to support and enhance the learning opportunities for students whether in or out of the classroom.

Beloit College's Approach to the Sophomore Year

The Sophomore-Year Initiatives Program is based on a foundation of the First-Year Initiatives Program, which begins with the students' arrival on campus. Students immediately join their chosen FYI seminars, taught by the faculty member who will be their academic advisor for two years. The week-long orientation program (New Student Days) combines an introduction to college life both in and out of the classroom. The seminar continues throughout the semester as a credit-bearing course with an interdisciplinary content. It also addresses students' transition from high school and home to college, academic and social integration, peer relationships, relationships with significant adults (e.g., the faculty advisor), and the value of a liberal education. Academic and student affairs have collaborated throughout the development and implementation of FYI/SYI. The co-directorship for each program is shared by a faculty member and the dean of students, which emphasizes the importance of this cooperation. Collaboration permeates all aspects of the programs from "advising lunches" for faculty development to establishing networks for student support (Batterman, Flanagan, & Ogurtsova, 2003, pp. 83-90).

The Sophomore-Year Initiatives Program continues the close interaction between students and faculty advisors, but with a strategy that differs from that of the First-Year Initiatives—sophomore students work more independently while receiving specific support from faculty and staff. Because it is during the sophomore year that students select their majors (and perhaps a minor), evaluate off-campus study options, and investigate experiential learning opportunities, Beloit College plans a series of programs not only to facilitate the decision-making process but also to make it serious, meaningful, and well thought out. Currently, the SYI events include:

1. Venture Grants
2. Welcome-Back Activities and Sophomore Dinner
3. Sophomore Retreat
4. Major Exploration and Declaration Fair
5. My Academic Plan (MAP)

Venture Grants

A venture grant project consists of entrepreneurial, self-testing activities in which a student or group of students attempts a project (academic or non-academic) that will benefit themselves, others, or the campus community. The application process is simple. A two- to three-page proposal sent to the Venture Grant Committee consists of a description of the project a student intends to complete over the summer or during the next academic year, a rationale for why this project should be funded, a detailed budget, and a time frame. The deadline for applications is late March. A month before the deadline, the co-directors of the Sophomore-Year program host the Venture Grant colloquium where first-year students receive all relevant information and meet with students who completed their projects the previous year. The Venture Grant committee consists of the co-directors of the FYI and SYI, as well as students who were previously awarded grants. The committee annually supports up to 10 projects with cash awards ranging from $500-$1500. Examples of previously funded projects include:

1. Participation in the Glenwood Springs Dance Festival and workshop. The student choreographed and directed her own show upon her return to campus.
2. Involvement in a two-month summer internship with the ministry of foreign affairs in Tbilisi, Republic of Georgia. This student served as a correspondent from Beloit College and conducted interviews with high-ranking government officials. While conducting the interviews, the student took pictures and then mounted an exhibition in a student-managed gallery in the Beloit campus center.
3. Acceptance of an opportunity at "Dad's Garage," an improvisational theater in Atlanta, GA, to study improv theater and directing. After returning to campus, the student applied what he learned by starting a theater group focused on mixed-media presentations. The group wrote original works that incorporated musicians, painters, sculptors, dancers, and poets. During one of the annual sophomore retreats, the student and his group introduced their new improv theatre skills to the students, faculty, and staff in attendance.

Welcome-Back Activities and Sophomore Dinner

Welcome-back activities are designed to reconnect students with their peers and advisor(s) and to facilitate the continuation of their academic and social integration into the institution. During the summer, students and parents or guardians receive a letter from the vice president for student affairs describing the sophomore slump and the resources available on campus to cope with this phenomenon as well as a brochure introducing, in greater detail, the components of the Sophomore-Year Initiatives Program. Early in September, each FYI seminar reunites for a sit-down dinner in a private dining room, where advisors can pass on information about sophomore events and urge students to begin their MAP (My Academic Plan) planning, especially if they have plans to study off campus. Representatives from the Field and Career Services and the International Education offices are also invited to share information about their opportunities and programs. Since starting the sit-down dinners, the number of students interested in doing internships and participating in study abroad programs has increased significantly.

Sophomore Retreat

The idea of the Sophomore Retreat came about as an attractive strategy to reconnect our most at-risk students and to re-introduce them to programs and opportunities, both on and off campus, at a strategic point in their undergraduate careers. This re-introduction includes confronting such issues as committing themselves to a major, exploring the possibilities for off-campus study in domestic or study abroad programs, and learning about potential career opportunities. Although these students are still our concern, we do not neglect those students who are on target for maximizing their Beloit College experience. Consequently, a two-day retreat open to all sophomore students scheduled in early November at a Wisconsin resort allows further investigation into academic opportunities, as well as internships and other field experiences. The retreat is intentionally timed when the students are most likely to experience the sophomore slump, and the workshop devoted exclusively to the sophomore slump is well attended. Special efforts are made to recruit or encourage those students most in need of the retreat to attend. Numerous presentations and discussions about study abroad opportunities through the International Education Office and off-campus study in the United States are a prominent part of the weekend. Beloit alumni are invited to attend the retreat and to lead workshops and discussions on career directions and planning. Entertainment and social activities foster an atmosphere for effective interaction among students, advisors, faculty, staff, and alumni.

Equally important, sophomores identify issues or concerns they have for the campus and are encouraged to develop action plans to address them. Outcomes from the process include a new coffee house called the Java Joint, the Café Series of live entertainment, recycling initiatives, campus gardens, prejudice reduction workshops, and extended library hours during exam week. After the sophomore retreat or through the process of retreat preparation, campus leaders often emerge and continue the work started at the retreat. One initiative where students emerged as powerful and influential leaders was undertaken several years ago to serve an identified campus and community need. This group of sophomore students formed the Beloit Interaction Committee (BIC). Simply put, these students felt the College was in a "bubble," and they sought to increase the interaction between students, the campus, and the greater Beloit community. Isolation from the community is sometimes cited by students as one reason for their desire to transfer. The group's efforts continue to pay dividends thanks to their success in building stronger and more collaborative relationships between the College and our students with city leaders, business people, and community development specialists. Student input and requests for ideas and support are regularly sought through public forums and placement on community committee assignments. Beloit students, faculty, staff, and members of the Beloit community regularly come together to discuss strategies for improving the relationship between college students and the community.

Major Exploration and Declaration Fair

At the end of March, right before the fall semester advising period, the Major Exploration and Declaration Fair takes place. A joint event of the FYI and SYI programs, the fair is a great opportunity for first-year students to explore possible fields of study and for sophomores to declare majors and minors. Our goal is to provide a fun, interactive, educational experience to help students with their decision-making process. All academic departments and programs are represented in the main dining hall in the campus center, which is equipped with computers and informational brochures to help sophomore students select the courses of study best suited to their particular needs. Activities at the fair also highlight opportunities and possibilities relating to studies both on and off campus, such as internships, field experiences, and domestic and study abroad programs. In addition, students are introduced to potential major scholarship opportunities such as the Rhodes, Fulbright, and Marshall scholarships and are encouraged to complete their academic plans (MAP). The fair provides a chance for advisors to meet their advisees in an informal atmosphere before the advising period and to provide their expert advice. For first-year students, this event is the chance to explore options and talk to faculty and student majors. Students who are ready to declare their majors or minors find it convenient to have the relevant faculty in one location.

My Academic Plan

The comprehensive academic planning process called "My Academic Plan" (MAP) is a system that helps sophomores plan their remaining years at Beloit in an effective and productive manner. On the first day of their FYI seminars, first-year students receive their MAP folder containing a series of documents and information relating to their Beloit experience (e.g., Values of a Liberal Education, Opportunities Available at and through Beloit, Off-Campus and Overseas Programs, Prepare at Beloit for Life after Beloit, and Questions to Ponder). During the sophomore year, students address these questions, rough out a plan of courses and activities for their junior and senior years, and provide their academic advisors with an accompanying rationale. The MAP is actually much more than a planning document, for it offers a recap of courses and activities, encourages future participation in on- and off-campus activities and programs, and suggests possibilities for post-college plans. When students set foot on campus, we teach them time management; when we introduce them to MAP, we teach them life management. MAP takes its theme from the concept of a road map for our students. They have a chance to choose a scenic view (i.e., study abroad, participation in an off-campus program or an internship) or the most direct route (i.e., just fulfilling the requirements). Advisors give suggestions and direct students, but it is up to students ultimately to decide which path to follow. Students work closely with advisors to develop a strategy for getting the most out of their college years with an eye toward starting graduate school or beginning a successful career. The goal of MAP is to ensure that our students have no regrets about missing opportunities when they walk across the stage on their graduation day.

Results of the Sophomore-Year Program

The First-Year Initiatives and the Sophomore-Year Initiatives programs together have had a substantial impact on the Beloit College campus. The benefits are apparent in the evaluations completed by students, faculty, and staff; in the wide variety of campus programs that have been developed; and in the general improvement of the campus climate. It is, however, impossible to attribute specific outcomes to one program or the other since together they form a continuum. When operating as intended, the programs permeate all aspects of an individual student's first two years at Beloit and have a significant impact on the activities of involved faculty and staff.

Although the focus of FYI/SYI was to introduce students to the learning environment at Beloit College, planners had hoped that retention would improve as a by-product of these two initiatives. To date, retention has improved but not as significantly as we might have anticipated. Beloit College's graduation rate has been increasing slightly over the past few years though it has not yet reached the goal of 80%. Our current graduation rate of 72% is approximately 6% higher than when these programs were introduced. The initiative for the programs, however, did not stem purely from a concern about attrition; rather, the motive was to introduce programs that would have a significant impact on our students' experiences at Beloit College. From this point of view, the programs have been very successful.

Perhaps the most obvious result of FYI/SYI is the fact that students are now clearly aware of the Beloit College academic requirements and, therefore, graduate on schedule. Although the requirements were never very complicated, the registrar used to receive telephone calls at the end of April from distraught parents demanding to know why their student knew nothing of a specific requirement that was now preventing his/her graduation. Today, these calls are rare and easily deflected. On their first day at Beloit, students receive a MAP folder, which includes a simple checklist of graduation requirements. Moreover, one part of MAP involves deciding which courses to take in order to satisfy these requirements.

It is difficult to finish degree requirements on schedule if students are still unsure of their majors in their junior year. Declaration of a major is the point when students become part of an academic department, transfer to a departmental faculty advisor, and truly become integrated into the academic life of the College. FYI/SYI advisors, the academic advising office, academic departments, and the Major Exploration and Declaration Fair all encourage entering students to try new courses and explore areas of interest purposefully, with a view to making a decision by the end of the sophomore year. Ten years ago, almost 50% of juniors had not declared their major; today only a handful of students are still undeclared as they finish their sophomore year.

MAP, however, has had other far-reaching results. The MAP process asks students to think about the purpose of their educations and encourages them to take advantage of the many opportunities available. While Beloit College students have always been active and done many interesting things, the process of conscious planning involved in MAP enables more students to fit a larger number of significant and worthwhile courses, activities, and experiences into their Beloit education. The addition of the international and experiential-learning expectations (Beloit College expects, but does not require, that students will do both) coincided with the advent of the sophomore dinners. As a consequence, the number of students applying for off-campus study (i.e., domestic and study abroad programs) has almost doubled from 73 students in 1995-96 to 144 students in 2004-05. Similarly, more students are actively seeking out experiential learning opportunities, such as internships and independent research projects. Altogether, MAP is helping students better prepare themselves for life after Beloit.

A very significant result of FYI/SYI is a greater emphasis on the importance of academic advising at Beloit College. For many years, academic advising has been one of the four criteria considered in faculty tenure decisions. During the last 10 years, its relevance has become almost universally accepted. For many new faculty, the programs provide the initiation into an understanding of the scope of academic advising as well as the skills and knowledge required by academic advisors. The process of getting to know and to care about a group of 15 students from the moment of their arrival on campus through their sophomore year helps new faculty quickly realize that many non-academic factors are important in a student's college success. This regular contact with their advisees causes faculty to understand that their role is not simply to help students choose their courses for the following semester but also to help advisees develop a grander scheme for their education. Additionally, faculty come to understand that they must be there to provide support, counsel, and encouragement as their advisees face the strains and crises of normal student life. This development of understanding is especially important for new faculty members who themselves attended large universities, since such faculty may not have had the experience of close advising relationships between faculty and students. Today, recently hired tenure-track faculty destined to become good advisors seek advice and support from fellow faculty and from members of the student affairs staff on how to offer appropriate assistance to their advisees as each new circumstance arises.

Another significant and unforeseen result of FYI/SYI is a general change in the campus climate. The divide between faculty and student affairs staff has narrowed significantly through regular collaboration on the organization and logistics of the programs and regular consultations about individual students. Faculty and staff now generally regard each other as colleagues united in a common goal: the well being of both individual students and Beloit College. This mutual knowledge, respect, and trust encourages further cooperation, which benefits the entire campus community.

It is important to encourage faculty advisors to expend the time and energy to connect with those students who are least responsive and most at risk of leaving. These students are less likely to approach their professors or use campus resources (e.g., Learning Resource Center, Field and Career Services). The students who are not academically integrated into college life are often the students who have not achieved social integration. They are alienated from the campus community, have few friends, feel separated ideologically, and even hold contempt for the surrounding town. Faculty advisors can have an impact on their social integration by encouraging them to explore their interests and become engaged in worthwhile activities, which may vary from participating in cultural events, sports, campus clubs, or intellectual discussions with friends, to volunteering within the Beloit community or becoming involved with college governance.

In order for academic advisors to be aware of their advisees' interests and needs, they must maintain regular contact with individual students. Beloit attempts to ensure this contact through its FYI and SYI programs. The vast majority of Beloit College faculty advisors do an excellent and conscientious job of maintaining this contact; nevertheless, some students continue to fall through the cracks. Our program continues to evolve through the use of assessment in planning, program development, and resource allocation as we work to eliminate these cracks and improve the quality of existing activities.

The Sophomore Retreat is the single most widely attended component of the SYI program so it has become the basis for much of our assessment efforts, especially since we make a significant effort to attract to the retreat those students who are most at risk of departure from campus. It is for that reason we have developed the following measurements of student-related issues between those who attend the retreat and those who do not. Specifically, we look at measurements that would help determine the academic and social integration of students, variables so important in determining student satisfaction. The measurements include academic and social suspension or dismissal, probation, voluntary withdrawal rates, connections with classmates and connections with faculty and staff. The evidence clearly demonstrates that those who attend the Sophomore Retreat have a significantly better chance of avoiding academic or social problems and are more likely to persist to graduation.

For example, our data suggest that students who attended the retreat were more likely to graduate from the College than those who did not attend (Figure 1). With the exception of 1998, students were far less likely to be suspended or dismissed from the College or placed on probation for academic reasons if they attended the retreat (Figures 2, 3, 4). Students were also less likely to withdraw from the College if they attended the retreat (Figure 5). The data clearly support our belief that the retreat is an important and positive element of our SYI program.

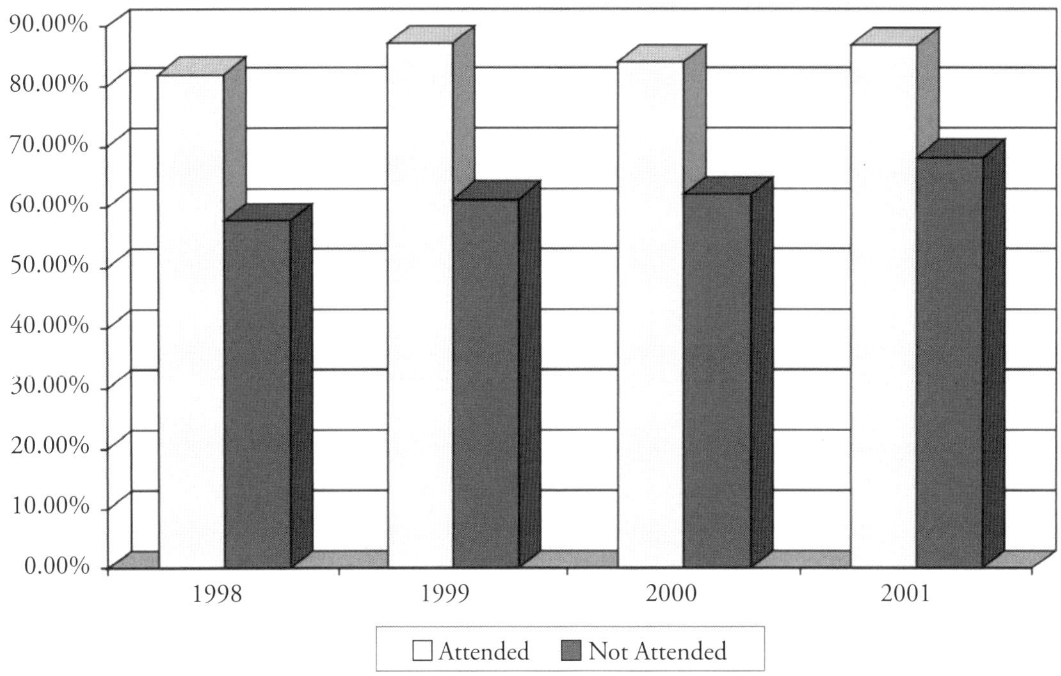

Figure 1. Graduation rates by attendance at Sophomore Retreat, 1998 – 2001 (Flanagan & Ogurtsova, 2006).

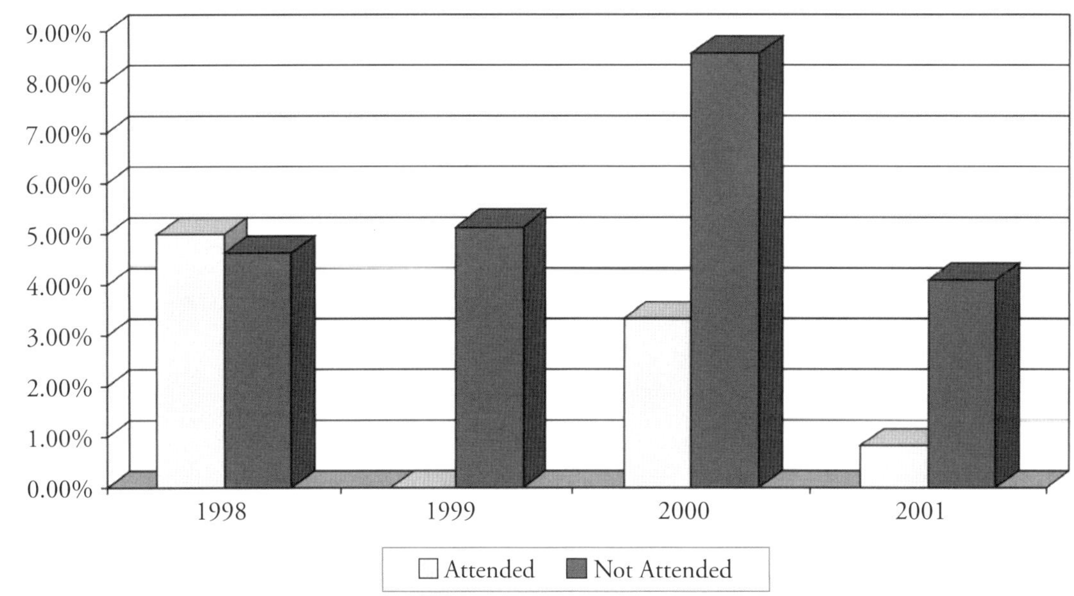

Figure 2. Academic suspensions by attendance at Sophomore Retreat, 1998 – 2001 (Flanagan & Ogurtsova, 2006).

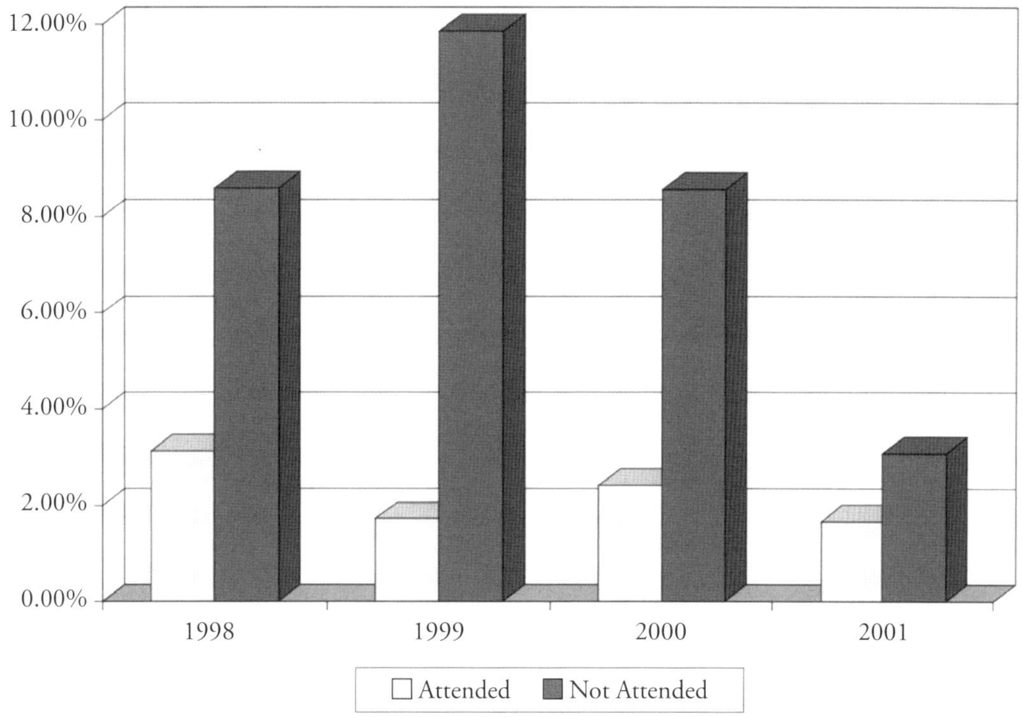

Figure 3. Academic dismissals by attendance at Sophomore Retreat, 1998 – 2001 (Flanagan & Ogurtsova, 2006).

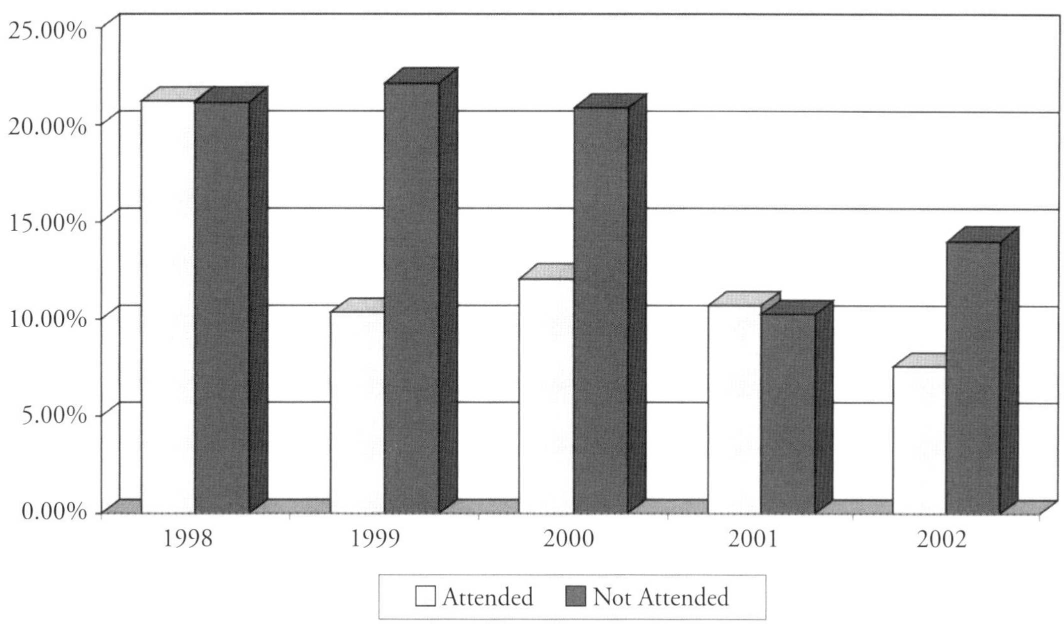

Figure 4. Academic probations by attendance at Sophomore Retreat, 1998 – 2001 (Flanagan & Ogurtsova, 2006).

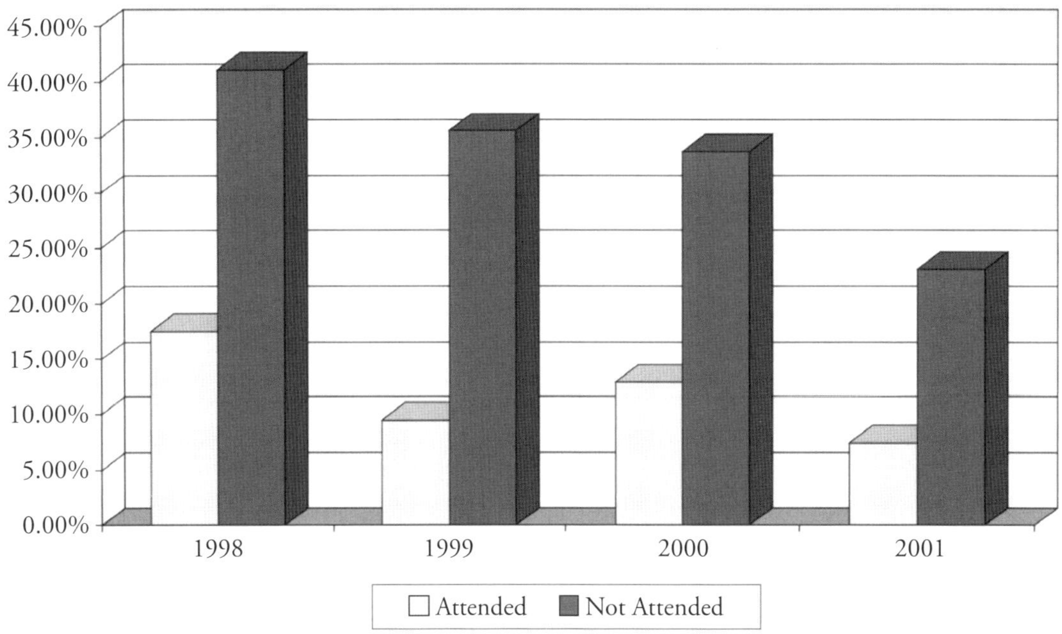

Figure 5. Withdrawals by attendance at Sophomore Retreat, 1998 – 2001 (Flanagan & Ogurtsova, 2006).

Challenges and Opportunities

Our assessment efforts suggest five key areas for growth and development of the SYI program. The first is the need for additional budgetary resources for our Venture Grants, speakers, retreat, and faculty/staff development and training. These are areas where additional financial resources will support the continued growth and expansion of the program to ensure students are better integrated into the academic and social environment both on and off campus.

Second, we must make even stronger and more intentional efforts to build the integration of our FYI and SYI programs to ensure a smoother transition from one program to the next. We believe this relationship is critical for meeting our educational, programmatic, and retention goals.

Third, we need to press the importance of ensuring that faculty who teach an FYI seminar can commit for the full two years expected of each seminar leader. Sabbaticals and leaves of absence during the second year can hinder student integration and may contribute to student dissatisfaction with their experience at Beloit.

Fourth, assessment efforts that measure faculty, staff, and student reactions to program goals need improvement, especially after each component of the program has been completed. These assessment efforts must be a part of a comprehensive assessment strategy where results are used for program changes, planning, and the allocation of scarce resources.

Finally, efforts must be made to develop a special sophomore-year curricular experience. Several ideas in the planning stages include sophomore-oriented courses or a specially designed activity similar to the New Student Days component of our FYI program in which sophomore students engage in an academic activity working closely with faculty, staff, and their peers on a special project in the local community.

Conclusion

While retention has definitely improved, the real impact of SYI has been the level to which these programs have become a part of the College's curricular and cocurricular fabric. They serve important educational and institutional needs on campus while providing many opportunities for close collaboration between faculty and staff, primarily the student affairs staff. When faculty and staff collaboration is institutionalized, as it is in this case, students experience a much more positive and responsive educational environment in which to learn, grow, and develop their full potential.

Finally, it is clear to the stakeholders of these two programs that their efforts have contributed to the development of a better, more comprehensive approach to the learning environment for first- and second-year students at Beloit College both in and out of the classroom. It is equally clear that graduation rates, although better, have not reached anticipated goals. It may take more time for the effects of these programs to be felt, but the reality is that retention is a very complex issue affected by many variables and factors. However, both the FYI and SYI programs serve as powerful and positive demonstrations that incorporating quality and innovative educational experiences for students into the curriculum and cocurriculum is a sound institutional strategy and investment.

References

Batterman, G., Flanagan, W. J., & Ogurtsova, O. (2003). Beloit College sophomore-year program. In M. K. Hemwall & K. C. Trachte (Eds.), *Advising and learning: Academic advising from the perspective of small colleges and universities.* (NACADA Monograph No. 8, pp. 83-90). Manhattan, KS: Kansas State University, National Academic Advising Association.

Chickering, A. W. (1969). *Education and identity.* San Francisco: Jossey-Bass.

Flanagan, W. J. (1991). *Sophomore retention: the missing strategy in small college retention efforts.* Unpublished doctoral dissertation, University of Wisconsin-Madison.

Flanagan, W. J., & Ogurtsova, O. (2006). *Ways to beat the "sophomore slump."* [Powerpoint Presentation] Beloit, WI: Beloit College. Retrieved June 28, 2007 from, http://www.beloit.edu/~syi/research/

Lemons, J. L., & Richmond, D. R. (1987). A developmental perspective of sophomore slump. *NASPA Journal*, 24, 15-19.

Lewis, T. J., & Jungman, R. E. (Eds.). (1986). *On being foreign: Culture shock in short fiction.* Yarmouth, ME: Intercultural Press.

National Institute of Education (1984). *Involvement in learning: Realizing the potential of American higher education.* Washington, DC: U.S. Department of Education.

Noel, L., Levitz, R., Saluri, D., & Associates. (Eds.). (1986). *Increasing student retention.* San Francisco: Jossey-Bass.

Pascarella, E. T., Terenzini, P. T., & Wolfle, L. M. (1986). Orientation to college and freshman year persistence/withdrawal decisions. *Journal of Higher Education, 57*, 153-174.

Terenzini, P. T., & Wright, T. M. (1987). Students' personal growth during the first two years of college. *The Review of Higher Education, 10*, 259-271.

Tinto, V. (1987). *Leaving college: Rethinking the causes and cures of student attrition.* Chicago, IL: University of Chicago Press.

Upcraft, M. L., Gardner, J. N., & Associates (1989). *The freshman year experience.* San Francisco: Jossey-Bass.

Chapter 5

The Sophomore Jump Program at Colorado College

Julie Tetley Stockenberg

Founded in 1874, Colorado College (CC), a private, four-year liberal arts college, is located on a 90-acre campus in downtown Colorado Springs near the base of the 14,110-foot Pikes Peak. Consistently ranked in the top tier in *U.S. News & World Report* for its academic excellence, CC is the only such college in the Rocky Mountain region. With a total enrollment of approximately 2,000 students, CC enrolls about 500 first-year students each new academic year. Best known for our innovative Block Plan, where students take and professors teach only one course at a time, CC offers a unique perspective on core classes and standard curriculum. CC creates small and supportive learning communities with every block and gives students the time to participate fully, without distractions. Our students come from every state in the nation and from more than 25 countries. They represent a wide range of ethnic, religious, and socioeconomic backgrounds, and they have interests as diverse as their backgrounds.

As reflected in our core values, members of the Colorado College community share a commitment to

- Honor the life of the mind as the central focus of our common endeavor
- Value all persons and seek to learn from their diverse experiences and perspectives
- Practice intellectual honesty and live with integrity
- Serve as stewards of the traditions and resources of Colorado College
- Nurture a sense of place and an ethic of environmental sustainability
- Encourage engagement and social responsibility at local, national, and global levels
- Seek excellence, constantly assessing our policies and programs

Along with the core values, the College's mission and strategic plan guide the development of new programs.

Colorado College, like other institutions, recognized it had some retention issues; however, with the implementation of specific programming for first-year students, CC found more of its students succeeding. This development led CC to focus its attention on the second college year. This chapter details the background surrounding the development of a sophomore-specific program, Sophomore Jump, at Colorado College. It continues with data on sophomore students, including qualitative results from focus groups and a survey of student mentors, and concludes by describing the various components of CC's Sophomore Jump program.

In 2000, CC introduced specific academic programs for first-year students. Taught across all academic disciplines at the college, the goals and objectives of the first-year seminars provide intentional opportunities for first-year students to adjust to the academic and social demands of college. The seminars also encourage students to develop a liberal arts mindset, increased intellectual curiosity, and a set of academic skills including critical reading of texts and analytic thinking. To support these goals, each seminar includes a substantial writing component, a research project, and an introduction to the College's academic resources.

Shortly after the creation of the first-year program, CC conducted an extensive retention study. Typically, retention studies suggest that each subsequent year of college should show half as many students departing. While first-year students were retained at higher rates, data from the CC study indicated that almost as many students left the college after their second year as they did after the first. In response to this curious finding and in an effort to increase the overall graduation rate, CC established the ad hoc Committee on Student Success.

At the same time the Committee on Student Success was making recommendations, the College authored a successful grant aimed broadly at institutional renewal. As a result, in 2003, the College acknowledged the need to improve academic advising and to concentrate more attention on students' first- and second-year experiences by establishing an office and director of First-Year and Sophomore Studies and Advising. One of the primary roles of the new director was to gather data about the needs of sophomore students and to develop sophomore-specific programs. Out of this new focus came the Sophomore Jump program.

Exploring the Experiences of Second-Year Students

Focus Group Data

In 2004, with the national data as the backdrop, Colorado College conducted a series of three small focus groups. These focus groups offered sophomores and juniors the opportunity to reflect on their sophomore year and share their insights. When establishing the focus groups, a deliberate attempt was made to invite students who were high-performing, engaged leaders of the campus and students who were underperforming and not engaged with the campus community. The response to our invitation to participate from the *disengaged* students was minimal. Although, the sample size of the three focus groups was small, totaling 15 students, analysis of the responses revealed four common themes: (a) a search for purpose and meaning; (b) questioning of personal identity; (c) increased commitment to friends, groups, academics, and activities; and (d) reduced motivation and apathy (Table 1).

Survey of First-Year Student Mentors

In addition to these focus groups, in an effort to better understand the experiences of second-year students, Colorado College surveyed second-, third-, and fourth-year students who serve as mentors for the first-year program. These student mentors are chosen by faculty and assigned to a first-year seminar class; they also work with students near the end of the first year to prepare them for what lies ahead. As part of their training, mentors discuss issues related to the sophomore year and are asked to reflect on their own experiences. Twenty-nine of the 35 student mentors (nine sophomores, six juniors, and 14 seniors) answered a questionnaire. Student mentors gave written responses to the following questions:

Table 1
Common Themes: Focus Group Data

Themes	Student Comments
Search for purpose and meaning	• "We're still figuring out what we're doing and that could be a long year of just kind of being in limbo." • "I expected it to be a lot like last year and it hasn't been." • "It was becoming part of the department and really, wandering upon a major and then feeling like, 'Oh yeah, this is going to give some sort of shape or form to the next 2½ years here.'"
Identity conflicts and formation	• "So while my grades don't reflect how much I learned because I had no confidence in myself, I learned a lot about me, I learned a lot about how to study, and what I need to do." • "I had this mid-college crisis where I just sat over the summer thinking about the things I was doing and where I want to be when I graduate and what I need to bring into my life and take out of my life to get there. So I think for me anyway, it's kind of this pivotal time when I asked, Well, here we are halfway. Now what needs to happen, or what do I want to get out of this place before I'm done." • "Sophomore year was a lot of soul searching for me"
Commitment (to friends, groups, activities, academics).	• "I'm not doing as many things as I did last year, but I'm twice as busy as I was last year ... more involved in just a couple of things where I have leadership roles." • "I think a lot of patterns and habits are formed sophomore year because I think a lot of kids experiment and party and kind of slack off freshman year and then you really see people go a couple different directions sophomore year."
Reduced motivation and apathy	• "The other sophomores and myself kind of just feel like kind of stuck this year, like going through the motions and not really feeling inspired or excited." • "I know a couple of people, and I can't explain why, but they've gone through periods of apathy where they just stop caring."

1. Reflect on your sophomore year—What helped you to feel that you had purpose and helped you to realize who you were (i.e., establish your identity)?
2. What are the major issues, needs, and/or tasks of sophomore students?
3. Have you ever heard of or experienced the "sophomore slump"? If so what are some characteristics of this stage of college development?

To the question *"What helped you to feel that you had purpose and helped you to realize who you were (establish identity) during the second year?"* mentors responses were similar to the earlier focus group findings. Mentors' responses highlight seven general themes: (a) structured opportunities for questioning values and personal identity, (b) goal setting, (c) discovery of one's passions, (d) declaration of a major, (e) assuming leadership roles, (f) building relationships with professors, and (g) solidifying friendships (Table 2).

Table 2
Student Responses to Developing Purpose in the Sophomore Year (n = 29)

Themes	Student Mentor Responses
Questioning values and personal identity	• "Taking classes that helped me take stock [of] values that I had not questioned in a while. Becoming involved in more social organizations and taking ownership for my potential majors." • "I don't really know how to answer this question. I feel like, if anything, I realized more that I really don't know exactly who I am and the person I was in high school is not the same person I am now. It was and still is a continuing journey to rediscover myself at this point in my life. I don't know everything, and I have a lot to learn about my life."
Setting goals	• "Goal setting and articulating that with friends. I need to explicitly state what my goals and purposes are for each class. Furthermore, I think talking to professors immediately and forming a relationship to work together through the course is important."
Discovering one's passions	• "Knowing what was most important to me in life and keeping school (during my sophomore slump moments) in perspective. Secondly, knowing also what subjects I am passionate about, good at, so I could include those in my sophomore year."
Assuming leadership roles	• "Also, finding a role as a leader among freshman and friends really helped me to continue to find myself and finalizing plans for studying abroad this fall."
Academic planning and declaring a major	• "Expanding my academic abilities and finding my niche in higher level classes as well as declaring my major." • "Lots of ups and downs: I was really trying to decide what I wanted to study and what I wanted to do with the rest of my time here (study abroad). I had lots of doubts as I got into the more difficult class (like organic chemistry)."
Building relationships with professors	• "Sophomore year was the most challenging in terms of motivation and desire. I think I was depressed mostly because I wasn't academically sure of what I wanted to study. Close relationships with professors helped make this an easier period. But sophomore year is definitely the hardest. I would recommend going abroad second semester sophomore year." • "I failed my first course sophomore year. I really had to search and see if CC was right for me. I didn't have homesickness first year, it hit second year. I wanted to leave. It helped to speak to Hispanic faculty. They helped me realize my strengths and options. I was told to go abroad. I went and decided to stay at CC."
Solidifying friendships	• "Friends—solidifying relationships was really important."

The survey of student mentors also asked, *what are the major issues, needs, and/or tasks of sophomore students?* Mentors responses indicate three general areas of concern: (a) pressure to declare a major, (b) need for social support of a campus community, and (c) reduced motivation (Table 3).

Table 3
Student Mentor Responses to Major Issues, Needs, or Tasks in the Sophomore Year (n = 29)

Issues, Needs, or Tasks	Mentor Responses
Pressure to declare a major	• "Dealing with pressure and expectations and feeling like the rest of my life has to be decided NOW!" • "Giving students the ability to explore and get to know departments they are interested in is key to their success. Also to keep them from completely being focused on partying and social life and losing the academic side."
Need for social support of a campus community	• "Re-evaluating social networks." • "There is the whole academic need of narrowing down an area of study, but I think that additionally sophomores need a lot of social support (psychological support). This may be because the 'fun intro' that characterizes freshman year is over, it's time to work, classes get harder, families get more distant, etc." • "I think it's hard for sophomores because it's the 'unspecial' year. Still underclassmen, but not freshmen, sophomores are kind of left out."
Reduced motivation	• "Some of the issues I think are feelings of being lost or overwhelmed, losing motivation to work as hard as you did before." • "Understanding that it's normal to feel exhausted/ uninterested, and that LIFE WILL GO ON."

Mentors were asked, *Have you ever heard of or experienced the sophomore slump? If so, what are some characteristics of this stage of college?* All respondents indicated that they had at least heard of the phenomenon. Table 4 lists student mentor descriptions of the sophomore slump, whether described in self or others (ranked in order of mention).

Both Colorado College's campus-based research and national research, demonstrates a need for the creation of a more intentional second-year experience for students. The data suggests seven main areas of focus when developing a second-year program including: (a) community building and class identity, (b) opportunities to interact with faculty outside of class, (c) active involvement and connection on campus including developmentally appropriate leadership opportunities, (d) encouragement of forward thinking (i.e., study abroad and internship opportunities), (e) critical self-assessment, (f) structured major/interest exploration, and (g) social networking. These seven areas guided the development of a new sophomore-specific program at Colorado College.

Table 4
Student Mentor Responses Defining the Sophomore Slump (n = 29)

Characteristics	Mentor Responses (in ranked order of mention)
Academic issues	Poor grades/academic disengagement, academic work is overwhelming, feeling stupid, unfulfilled by classes, not wanting to go to class, not doing well, not doing the work, apathy for academic work, lack of motivation and interest in studies, taking required courses that one is not passionate about
Doubts about "institutional fit"	Considering transferring/doubts that CC is the right school, wondering why one is at CC (or college), actually taking time off, strong desire to just go have adventures
Mental health issues	Depression and its symptoms (e.g., tiredness, lethargy)
Lack of direction	Feeling lost, doubts about what to do with life, not knowing what to do in general; learning a lot but not able to act
Feelings of isolation	Feeling like one has no friends, feeling lonely, feeling of not fitting in, feeling like staying inside all the time, difficulty finding friends in already formed groups, homesickness
Excessive partying	Partying excessively, heavy drinking, substance abuse
Anxiety about decisions	Anxiety about anything from social life to decision making
Lack of excitement	College is dull; all is more of the same, being in a rut, things aren't exciting
Lack of vision for the future	Not being able to see "the light at the end of the tunnel"
Focus on socializing	Focus on non-academic activities and friends to the exclusion of classes
Lack of self-esteem	Lower self-esteem
Desire for change	Not wanting to continue with first-year path and mentality
Pressure of expectations	Feeling like the rest of one's life must be decided immediately
Self-actualization	Realizing that one needs to satisfy oneself and be self-motivated, rather than doing everything to please others

Development of a Second-Year Program at Colorado College

Creation of a New Director

The first step toward developing a second-year program at Colorado College was the creation of the director of First-Year and Sophomore Studies and Advising. A large portion of the director's job is to create specific programming for each class as appropriate to their yearly progress, with the aim to improve students' collegiate experience. These initiatives include:

- Enhanced advising and programming in conjunction with the first-year program including interviews/survey of all students in the first-year class to assess the faculty/student advising relationship
- Follow-up programming in the sophomore year to ensure that students are establishing goals and are ready to declare an appropriate major; facilitate the move to the major department

In addition, the director monitors the academic progress of first- and second-year students, refers students to various campus academic resources (e.g., Writing Center and Quantitative Reasoning Center), and is instrumental in developing and implementing programs that assist students with their educational planning and progression to graduation. The director also serves as a supplementary advisor, within a faculty-based advising system, for first- and second-year students. The advantage of this shared advising system is that it allows the College to keep a valued faculty/student relationship, which proves beneficial to student retention while providing additional resources for both the faculty advisor and first- and second-year students. Outside the support for students, the director acts as a resource for faculty advisors and coordinates a complete series of workshops for new faculty advisors.

Survey of Existing Campus Programs

The director of First-Year and Sophomore Studies and Advising began by gathering information about existing campus events and programs. This process revealed a number of existing resources and programs at Colorado College; however, these were not packaged as specific programs for second-year students. These events/programs included Campus Activities Night, the Scholarship and Fellowship Fair, the International Opportunities and Study Abroad Fair, and the Internships and Job Fair. In addition, many academic departments sponsor lectures on campus. These lectures engage students intellectually and expose them to research opportunities and a world beyond college. These opportunities are beneficial for any student but are developmentally appropriate opportunities for second-year students and were, therefore, the beginning of the Sophomore Jump program at Colorado College.

A Balance of Academic and Social Components

At Colorado College, one of the greatest challenges to creating a second-year program is balancing the social and academic components. After determining what already existed, and with the seven areas of focus mentioned above in mind, the director identified gaps in programming. Various colleges, including Beloit College and Colgate University, served as useful models in creating additional components of the Sophomore Jump program (see chapters 4 and 7 in this monograph, respectively). It became evident that a comprehensive program for second-year students would require collaborative efforts of academic and student affairs.

Partnerships with Academic and Student Affairs

When developing a new program or campus initiative, building support from the upper-level administration is key. During the beginning stages of program development, the director of First-Year and Sophomore Studies and Advising determined who the primary and secondary stakeholders were for a sophomore-specific program and began conversations with individuals across academic and student affairs departments. With financial resources from a grant, and support from the Dean's office, cultivating grass roots support and partnerships was a next important step.

At Colorado College, two important partnerships between academic and student affairs contributed to the development of a second-year program—one with residence life and the other with career services. The first is a partnership between Residential Life and the Office of First-Year and Sophomore Studies and Advising. The residential life coordinator (a master's level professional) supervises the primarily sophomore residence hall and spends approximately 10 hours per week focusing on sophomore program development and support. In addition, the student residential assistants who live in this residence hall receive targeted training about the developmental needs and characteristics of sophomore students and serve as partners in the educational process.

One product of this collaboration is the quarterly *Sophomore Connection* newsletter. Articles in the *Sophomore Connection* focus on career decision making, academic planning, internships, academic skills, and other topics of interest to sophomores. Copies of the newsletter can be found on Colorado College's *Your Sophomore Year* web site: http://www.coloradocollege.edu/academics/sophomore/sophconnection.asp

In addition to placing the newsletter on the web site, each sophomore receives a copy from his or her resident assistant.

Sophomore Living-Learning Community

The collaboration between Residential Life and the Office of First-Year and Sophomore Studies and Advising, along with leadership from the Partnership for Civic Engagement, also led to the creation of a sophomore-specific living-learning community in 2005. The community draws on the model of Freshman Interest Group (FIG) housing and other residentially based learning communities. The students who live in this residential area enroll in a sociology course entitled, Multiculturalism and Democracy. In a community-based learning course, students put theory into practice, not only in their own residential community but in the larger Colorado Springs community. In addition to the coursework, students engage in a series of workshops designed to enhance civic competencies and leadership skills. As Anderson and Schreiner (2000) note,

> By asking sophomores to commit to service, we are increasing the potential for their learning experiences to engage their whole person. In addition, by focusing beyond themselves, sophomores can derive meaning and purpose in a year that may have otherwise been only endured as a necessary step to graduation. (p. 61)

This living-learning community engages second-year students in a process of critical self-reflection and application of theory.

Partnership with the Career Center

The other important partnership is with the Career Center, which provides resources for students to explore interests, personality characteristics, and values. It also offers two commonly used self-assessments: (a) the Holland Self-Directed Search (SDS) and (b) the Myers-Briggs or TypeFocus™ personality inventory. The SDS helps students to understand more about themselves and how their individual skills, interests, and abilities relate to future career choices and majors. Holland's (1994) theory argues that most people can be loosely categorized with respect to six types: (a) Realistic, (b) Investigative, (c) Artistic, (d) Social, (e) Enterprising, and (f) Conventional. Occupations, work environments, and college majors/minors can also be loosely classified by the same categories. The TypeFocus Inventory™, based upon the Myers-Briggs personality typology, focuses on identifying the strengths, preferences, and natural tendencies of the individual and helps students to clarify their values, skills, and interests.

When used appropriately, these self-assessments empower students to discover more about themselves and help to bring focus, meaning, and purpose to their academic studies during the second year. Based on this understanding, a series of workshops were added to the Sophomore Jump program. Held in the afternoon in the primarily sophomore residential hall, the first workshop series consists of four topics: (a) Self-Awareness (i.e, TypeFocus™ and Holland Self-Directed Search); (b) Putting the Pieces Together to Narrow the Focus: Connecting Your Self-Assessment with Potential Majors; (c) Exploring Majors, presented by a panel of students from various departments; and (d) Exploring Careers, Internship Opportunities. In addition to this series, which focuses on exploration of self, majors, and careers, a skill-based workshop series (Are You Ready for Primetime?) prepares students for part-time jobs or other work experience. This series of workshops offers second-year students the opportunity to develop a professional resume and to prepare and practice interview skills. These two workshop series provide a structured way for second-year students to learn more about themselves and their interests, leading to the declaration of a major, and to prepare to study abroad and complete internships.

Sophomore Welcome Back Luau

Colorado College kicks off the year with a Sophomore Luau. Faculty who taught in the first-year experience program are invited to reunite with their students at the Luau. The President welcomes the students back and invites them to take advantage of the multitude of events that are specifically for second-year students. Complete with a Hawaiian buffet dinner, a live Hawaiian band, and a sophomore class gift, the Sophomore Luau is expensive but sets the tone for the second year by letting students know that they are important and not forgotten. In the past two years, more than half of the second-year students attended the Sophomore Luau.

Faculty-Sophomore Dinner Series

One of the most successful events in Colorado College's Sophomore Jump program is the Sophomore/Faculty Dinner Series. This dinner series provides an opportunity for second-year students to form relationships with faculty outside the traditional classroom environment and encourages them to continue to explore majors. Once a month, second-year students are invited to participate in a formal dinner (including sparkling cider) held in the Presidential Board Room. The featured faculty member presents his/her intellectual autobiography and engages second-year students in conversation about the majors and minors they advise. Dinners are limited to the first 20 students to respond to the e-mail invitation, and generally there is a waitlist of students who are eager to attend. Following the dinner, one student commented,

> I really enjoyed the dinner. I had a great time listening to the professor as he described some of the things he's done and how he came to be who he is. His stories and slides were both entertaining and inspiring. I think it is a great idea and allows students to get to know fellow sophomores and faculty better and to explore possible majors.

Departmental Events for Prospective Majors

At Colorado College, some departments host events for students who are interested in majors in their discipline. The economics department hosts a "coming in" party for students who have recently or are strongly considering declaring economics as their major. Faculty talk about their areas of research; alums share their perspective about how the major contributed to their current jobs; juniors and seniors give hints about how to progress through the major successfully and share their upcoming thesis projects. This welcome party helps students better understand the expectations of the major and feel part of a departmental community. The chemistry and political science departments host ice cream socials for any first- and second-year students who have taken at least two courses in the department. The upper-class students and faculty talk with prospective majors about what it is like to be a major in their department.

The One-Day Sophomore Workshop

Similar to Beloit College's sophomore retreat, in 2004 Colorado College began a one-day Sophomore Jump workshop for second-year students. Prior to attending the workshop, students are asked to complete the TypeFocus™ and Holland Self-Directed Search. The day begins with an explanation of the results of the two self-assessments and an opportunity for students to ask questions about their results. This process is followed by a progressive majors lunch where students rotate to different tables where alums, faculty, and upper-class students represent the various majors/minors offered at Colorado College. Students begin by eating their salad at one table, their entrée at another, and their dessert at a third table, exploring three majors/minors during the meal. The day ends with three breakout sessions where students explore study abroad, internships, and community opportunities. In the busy lives of students, having a structured way to complete all of this in one day is attractive.

Sophomore-Specific Advising

Light (2001) writes, "Good advising may be the single most underestimated characteristic of a successful college experience" (p. 81). During the sophomore year, academic advisors are positioned to pose questions that will push students to think about an academic plan and the relationship of their academic work to their personal lives. Advising students toward courses that engage them in self-actualization and reflection can be particularly valuable for second-year students. Often courses with these components exist in the philosophy or psychology departments. Engaging students in conversation about the meaning and value of the liberal arts and connecting students' goals with the mission and core values of the college is particularly valuable for second-year students. At Colorado College, the director of First-Year and Sophomore Studies and Advising serves as a supplementary advisor for first- and second-year students and meets with as many as 250 students over the course of the year to assist students in making these connections and creating an academic plan for their future studies.

Packaging and Marketing the Product

Packaging and marketing Colorado College's Sophomore Jump program is very important. The millennial generation expects a colorful, interactive product. Second-year students may feel that they are not as important as they were when they first entered the college. Sometimes they are referred to as the middle child. At Colorado College, we dispel this belief by greeting them with a colorful and complete program that is specific to second-year students. Colorado College's Sophomore Jump program is illustrated in a neon green, foldout flyer with frogs covering the publication. In addition, a sophomore-only listserv proves to be a very effective way of informing students and encouraging their attendance at Sophomore Jump events.

Many colleges have created a sophomore-specific web pages like Colorado College's *Your Sophomore Year* page (www.coloradocollege.edu/academics/sophomore), which provides a forum to advertise sophomore-specific opportunities and offers resources that are appropriate for second-year students. One of the most valuable resources on this web page is a section called *What Can I Do With a Major In...* This resource is available for purchase from the University of Tennessee at Knoxville's Career Center and can be modified to fit the institution and loaded on the college's web site. For each academic major, appropriate career areas, potential employers, and strategies are complied on a printable chart. In addition, the site provides links to academic associations and career sites for each major. Students feel empowered to pursue their major areas of interest when they are able to understand and articulate what they plan to do after college with the major.

Like many colleges and universities across the nation, Colorado College has a strong student government organization with class officers. These student leaders have been helpful in determining what will work on our campus. A number of the Sophomore Jump events are cosponsored with the sophomore class officers. The officers help to advertise and to build interest in the program and events.

Next Steps

A formal assessment of the Sophomore Jump program has not been conducted; however, plans for assessment are underway. Informal feedback indicates that students appreciate the structured opportunities to explore interests and majors and feel a sense of connection as a result of the Sophomore Jump events. As we continue to expand the program, we hope to increase the number and variety of academic components within the Sophomore Jump program.

Conclusion

Due to a vast amount of research conducted on first-year students, most colleges and universities across the nation developed first-year programs to assist students in their transition to college. The result of frontloading our efforts is a rise in first-year retention rates and an improved experience for first-year students. Second-year students have different but equally important needs and transitions. Upon their return to college, without a sophomore-specific program, second-year students may feel a sense of abandonment. The novelty of college has worn off, and second-year students begin to question their own values, identity, social groups, academic areas of interest, and reason for continuing college. Although more research is needed, it has become apparent that second-year students benefit from a balance of challenge and support as they journey toward what Baxter Magolda (1999) calls self-authorship, "the ability to reflect upon one's beliefs, organize one's thoughts and feelings in the context of, but separate from, the thoughts and feelings of others, and literally make up one's own mind" (p. 6). A sophomore-specific program, like Colorado College's Sophomore Jump, designed around the specific needs and characteristics of second-year students will enhance the experience for students and give them the support they need to progress to their junior year and graduation.

References

Anderson, E., & Schreiner, L. A. (2000). Advising for student success. In L. A. Schreiner & J. Pattengale. (Eds.), *Visible solutions for invisible students: Helping sophomores succeed* (Monograph No. 31, pp. 55-65). Columbia, SC: University of South Carolina, National Resource Center for The First-Year Experience and Students in Transition.

Baxter Magolda, M. B. (1999). *Creating contexts for learning and self-authorship: Constructive-developmental pedagogy.* Nashville, TN: Vanderbilt University Press.

Holland, J. L. (1994). *Self-directed search.* Odessa, FL: Psychological Assessment Resources.

Light, R. (2001). *Making the most of college: College students speak their minds.* Cambridge, MA: Harvard University Press.

Chapter 6

Year 2 Kennesaw: The Sophomore Experience at a Public Metropolitan University

Edward K. Chan

In 2003, Kennesaw State University (KSU) initiated the Sophomore-Year Experience program in order to address the issues experienced by KSU sophomore students: finding a place and identity in the campus and academic culture; pursuing a degree in an intentional and knowledgeable way; and improving retention, progression, and graduation rates. The program has since been renamed "Year 2 Kennesaw: The Sophomore Year-Experience" (Y2K) program.

The specific goals of the program are to help sophomores transition smoothly from the first to the second year, connect to their academic major, navigate the general education sequence, take advantage of campus programs and resources, monitor and reflect on academic progress, and continue to the junior year and toward a degree. To fulfill those goals, we developed three programs: (a) Sophomore Peer Leaders, (b) Major Mentors, and (c) UpperCLASS (sophomore learning communities).

Year 2 Kennesaw differs from some other sophomore programs by its location in an academic department and by its lack of a defined operating budget. Being located in an academic department has definite advantages (i.e., access to the curriculum) but also disadvantages (i.e., restrictions on state-provided funds). This situation has necessitated a collaborative spirit, and if there is one principle that underlies all our efforts, it has been working with other programs across campus, in both student and academic affairs, in order to create support structures for sophomores.

KSU's student population is typical of a comprehensive state university located on the outskirts of a metropolitan area: mostly commuting and nontraditional students. As such, our second-year students do not necessarily possess a clear identity as "sophomores." Our students also tend to have substantial off-campus commitments (mostly working full-time or part-time jobs) that limit the time they can or want to spend on campus. This chapter describes three sophomore initiatives we have developed in the context of this type of institution. The chapter also identifies issues associated with each initiative and makes recommendations for similar institutions.

KSU Profile and the Evolution of Y2K

Institution

KSU is a public university within the University System of Georgia located about 30 minutes away from downtown Atlanta, serving the northwestern metropolitan Atlanta region. Of the 35 institutions comprising the system, KSU is currently the third largest overall and one of 13 in the "State University" category. Core values for this type of institution include service to a specific area of the state, emphasis on teaching and learning (including developmental studies), a "general education program supporting a variety of disciplinary, interdisciplinary, and professional academic programs at the baccalaureate level, with selected master's and educational specialist degrees" (Board of Regents, 2006). KSU emphasizes undergraduate education with a limited number of graduate degree programs: "Effective teaching and learning are central institutional priorities. Service and research that strengthen teaching and address the public's interests are important supportive priorities" (Kennesaw State University, 2006).

Students

Institutional research reports that KSU enrolled 18,556 students in fall 2005, 32% of whom were part-time with an average undergraduate age of 25 and 21% of whom (3,815) were sophomores (30-60 credit hours). Housing was first offered in 2002, but the overwhelming majority of students commute to campus (approximately 88% in fall 2005); nevertheless, about half of all full-time, first-year students lived on campus in fall 2005. Almost half of KSU's first-year students work at least 20 hours a week and about one third work more than 30 hours ("Graduate with A's," 2005). KSU's Center for Institutional Effectiveness reports that "[b]eyond the freshman classification, three-fourths of KSU's sophomores, juniors, and seniors were nontraditional and only one-fourth were traditional in age and full-time enrollment status" (2004, p. 4). Part of this statistic represents a pattern of traditional-aged students who drop to part-time status (often in favor of working), stop out, or drop out altogether after their first year at KSU. For example, the percentage of full-time students who enrolled in 1999 dropped from 100% to 85% in the sophomore year and eventually to 60% in the sixth year ("Graduate with A's"). Whereas the first-year class was overwhelmingly traditional-age (3,348) as compared to nontraditional (1,420) in fall 2006, the sophomore class was primarily nontraditional (2,201 vs. 1,705 traditional).

Though this needs to be researched more definitively, the student culture at KSU seems to value employment over study, which parallels longstanding trends in higher education nationally (Horn & Malizio, 1998). Even our students who do remain enrolled full-time gravitate toward the identity of "employees who study" rather than "students who work" (Horn & Malizio, p. 2). As at similar institutions (i.e., serving a predominantly nontraditional, commuting student population), KSU students often place work first and fit college education around it. In some cases, these priorities come from the need to support dependents; in others, they support a lifestyle chosen by the student. Regardless of the reason, KSU student culture has evolved such that it all but validates heavy workloads as well as a "parking lot – classroom – parking lot" mentality, which discourages on-campus extracurricular activity. To some degree, this is a remnant of KSU's days as a community college in the late 1960s and much of the 1970s. Although the culture is becoming more campus oriented with the introduction of residential facilities and the increased presence of traditional-age students, at present, the culture makes it difficult to appeal to students' time outside the classroom. As Evenbeck, Boston, DuVivier, and Hallberg (2000) note, with significant commitments off campus, the experience of sophomore commuters is more complicated than during their first year.

Given the above characteristics, the nature of KSU's student population confounds the traditional idea of a student's four-year progression through the undergraduate curriculum: first year, sophomore year, junior year, senior year.

Birth of a Sophomore Program

KSU has had a long-running first-year program, with the inaugural first-year seminar (KSU 1101) being offered in 1983. With strong support from the former President Betty L. Siegel, KSU 1101 has grown to become a standard offering with 75 sections in fall 2006. KSU piloted a learning communities program, Communities for LeaArning SuccesS (CLASS), in fall 2000 with eight communities, and it has grown to currently more than 50 communities each fall. Current learning communities typically consist of 25 students who enroll in linked sections of KSU 1101 and two general education courses. Since 2005, the institution has made it a requirement for all full-time, first-year students with fewer than 15 credit hours to enroll in either the first-year seminar or a learning community (residential students are required to register for a learning community). Both KSU 1101 and CLASS have been recognized in *U.S. News & World Report's* America's Best Colleges: KSU 1101 was named a "program to look for" in the 2005 and CLASS was honored in 2006.

Building on the success generated by its first-year programs, KSU decided to initiate a sophomore program. Though retention has historically been an issue and a concern, the program evolved out of the institution's commitment to enabling student success. At the same time, it was becoming clear that student success issues extend beyond the first year (Pattengale & Schreiner, 2000). The first year is clearly an important time of transition and has received considerable attention at colleges and universities. However, many experts have recognized the need to extend support structures into subsequent years (Flanagan, 1991; Schreiner & Pattengale, 2000). Research on sophomores and sophomore programs is limited (though growing), but researchers suggest that "[i] nstitutions may be on the road to reducing first-year attrition, but without providing ongoing programs, services, and support to sophomores, efforts seem to be only postponing the inevitable until the end of the sophomore year" (Pattengale & Schreiner p. vi). Some of the literature points to advising/career selection (Anderson & Schreiner, 2000) and social and academic integration into the campus culture (Flanagan, 1991; Juillerat, 2000) as prominent issues that face sophomores. Both a sense of these pressures and a commitment to enabling student success led to the next logical step after the first year.

In spring 2003, KSU conducted a national search for a director of the Sophomore-Year Experience program. The institution chose to locate the director position in an academic department; thus, the position also carried with it teaching duties in the general education program. The program and director are housed in the Department of University Studies, which also houses the First-Year Experience programs (KSU 1101 and CLASS), the Senior-Year Experience program (which offers an elective senior-year seminar), the Honors program, learning support courses, the ESL Center, the recently launched Supplemental Instruction program, and the Center for Student Leadership (administered jointly with Student Success and Enrollment Services, KSU's student affairs division). The department evolved from being strictly a learning support department into a home for various programs that actively support students in achieving academic success. (As it would turn out, these other programs have provided useful resources and collaborations for Y2K.) In 2005, University Studies became the sole department in the newly created University College. The College oversees the general education curriculum, advising, and special initiatives such as the American Democracy Project (sponsored by the American Association of State Colleges and Universities, AASCU).

Early in the development of the program, a deliberate decision was made not to pursue a sophomore-specific course parallel to KSU 1101. While such a course would provide a way to address sophomores directly, it was felt that a sophomore course would be too difficult to get into the curriculum. In addition, KSU students are already overloaded with credit hours, and the HOPE scholarship program in Georgia, which provides free tuition to students who maintain a 3.0 GPA, has a cap on the number of credit hours a student may attempt. A few degree programs do not even have space for free electives.

Working from within an academic department provides definite advantages—for example, direct access to the curriculum and connections with other academic departments. However, this situation also poses particular obstacles. In the midst of a system-wide budget crunch, it is also difficult to secure funding for fledgling programs from a shrinking allocation to academic affairs. Unlike in student affairs divisions, the University System of Georgia places strict restrictions on spending in academic departments; thus, we are limited in our ability to do things as simple as providing food and refreshments at events. It is also difficult to offer programming of a social nature. Certainly, this situation requires flexibility, creativity, and a spirit of collaboration. Within this context, we developed the following three programs to help our sophomore students succeed at KSU: (a) Sophomore Peer Leaders, (b) Major Mentors, and (c) UpperCLASS Sophomore Learning Communities.

Sophomore Peer Leaders Program

Program Specifics

A recurring issue for sophomores is the lack of attention by the institution, especially after the extensive support structures offered in the first year (Evenbeck et al., 2000). Boivin, Fountain, and Baylis (2000) suggest that "[c]reating earlier opportunities to take responsibility for others and events seems to assist sophomores in finding their own way, helping them establish a sense of competence" (p. 6). The Sophomore Peer Leaders program was developed to give a limited number of sophomores such a role. Like other peer mentoring programs, the Sophomore Peer Leaders program draws on students' own experiences to help mentor other students. We first piloted the program during the fall 2004 semester. In spring 2004, KSU 1101 instructors were asked to nominate students who they felt successfully transitioned into the first year of college life (not necessarily tied to academic achievement). These students were invited to join the program, which would place them in classrooms with KSU 1101 instructors to provide a resource on first-year student issues at KSU for both students and instructors. Although Y2K does not have a program operating budget, this first group of peer leaders was hired using money budgeted for student workers in the Department of University Studies, providing a small and largely nominal stipend from departmental funds. Because some of KSU's academic majors do not provide much room for free electives and because students often want to conserve the number of credit hours applied to the HOPE Scholarship, we decided not to offer course credit for the experience. Each peer leader and assigned instructor worked out a formal set of expectations on both sides (e.g., number of classes for the peer leader to attend, presentation opportunities based on the peer leader's interests). In this incarnation, the program focused on developing mentoring relationships between the sophomore and the instructor (ideally, the one who nominated her or him), and each pair determined the nature of the peer leader's role in the classroom. Since this was also the pilot offering of the program, we wanted to see the variety of roles played by each peer leader in the classroom as developed by each pairing of peer leader and instructor, in order to guide development of the program.

The following year, we incorporated leadership training through the Center for Student Leadership's (CSL's) existing three-tiered student leadership program, LINK (Leaders IN Kennesaw). In April 2005, nominees were invited by their KSU 1101 instructors to make a formal application to the Sophomore Peer Leaders program that includes a letter of interest and a recommendation by a member of the faculty other than the nominator. These students would then complete the first tier of the LINK program (Emerge). Applications were also invited from second-semester first-year students who had completed LINK Emerge training and had also completed KSU 1101 during the previous fall semester. Applicants were interviewed and then selected based on their understanding of the philosophy of KSU 1101 as a first-year seminar as well as their leadership skills. Toward the end of the spring semester, each peer leader was paired with a KSU 1101 faculty member to develop a working relationship and provide input on a KSU 1101 syllabus for the fall semester. Peer leaders received further training during the summer to develop classroom and curricular strategies.

In general, peer leader duties include the following:

- Attending a substantial number of classes with the instructor, ranging from each class for the first quarter of the semester to one class a week for the entire semester to every class
- Leading community-building activities
- Providing an extra support structure to students enrolled in KSU 1101 beyond and apart from the faculty member and classmates by being available outside the classroom
- Meeting and communicating regularly with the KSU 1101 faculty member to coordinate involvement in the course
- Meeting with the program director at the beginning, middle, and end of the fall semester to report on their activities and provide feedback on the program

The following benefits were outlined for students who participated in the Sophomore Peer Leaders program:

- *Leadership training.* Beyond the skills developed in Emerge, students can continue to build on their leadership training in the LINK program to earn a certificate in ethical leadership.
- *Connecting with other students.* Students have the opportunity to develop relationships with other peer leaders as well as the KSU 1101 students with whom they are working.
- *Faculty mentorship.* Students are able to develop a close relationship with a faculty member and gain a perspective of a course from the "other side" (especially beneficial for students considering teaching as a profession).
- *Institutional accolade.* Students are officially recognized for their service during KSU's First-Year Student Convocation.

Issues

While the peer leaders program offers a clearly defined way for sophomores to become engaged with the institution in a meaningful way, it only involves a limited number of them. Moreover, KSU already had a well-established leadership program (LINK), which provided the best platform for training students to help lead first-year students in the KSU 1101 classroom. The value of the experience as a vehicle for student leadership training soon overshadowed the original intent of the program to simply re-engage sophomores through reflection on their own experience while providing a resource to first-year students. In the pilot version, the Sophomore Peer Leaders program emphasized self-reflection on the part of the sophomores, which happened to fulfill a need in the first-year seminar, as opposed to student leadership qualities. However, leadership—especially personal initiative and community-building skills—rose to the top as the primary functions of the peer leaders. At the same time, it was difficult to restrict the program only to sophomores—second-semester first-years, juniors, and seniors also expressed interest in the program. Thus, we decided to make the peer leaders program open to all students and fold it into the LINK program. As a result, the program is now housed solely in CSL.

Major Mentors Program

Program Specifics

As many as half the fall 2005 entering class of full-time, first-year students at KSU had not declared a major ("Graduate with A's," 2005). Moreover, of the full-time, first-year students who enrolled at KSU in fall 2003, a third of the undeclared first-year students dropped out (as compared to a fifth of first-year students who had declared majors) and an even higher percentage of those who were undeclared dropped out after two years ("Graduate with A's"). We designed Major Mentors as a way to help students transition smoothly into an academic major during their sophomore year. The program pairs a sophomore protégé with a senior or junior mentor in the sophomore's declared or intended academic major. The mentor makes a formal commitment to work with the protégé and is enrolled in either the Honors program or in the Senior-Year Experience seminar, KSU 4401. Additionally, the mentor receives training through KSU's Odyssey Peer Mentor program, run by the KSU Student Development Center. The pair initially meets at a kickoff banquet and then four more times over the course of a semester to discuss the particularities of the major, drawing on the knowledge and experience the mentor has gained during her or his undergraduate career. Mentors relate their perspective on what it means to be, for example, a psychology major; what they plan to do with their major after graduation; what they wish they would have known about their major as sophomores or juniors; and so forth.

KSU students often take advantage of informal advising from fellow students, which often devolves into which professor is "best" or "easiest." We tried to formalize this process by giving it form and substance. Through the mentor relationship, sophomore protégés can become more self-reflective and informed about their decision in choosing a major. For those students having trouble deciding on a major, the Major Mentors program can provide them a window into what a particular academic major entails.

Learning outcomes for the Major Mentors program are defined as follows:

- Students participating as protégés in Major Mentors will settle into an academic program thoughtfully and purposefully. Activities include:
    - Mapping out remaining courses up to graduation
    - Receiving and reviewing an annotated transcript detailing experiences in each course provided by the mentor
- Students participating as protégés in Major Mentors will connect socially with their peers. A mentor and a protégé meet at least four times (plus the kick-off banquet) for at least 30 minutes each time during the course of a semester.
- Students participating as protégés in Major Mentors will understand the opportunities for experiential learning within the major sponsoring the community. The mentor and protégé discuss information about opportunities for cooperative education, service-learning, and internships with mentor.

Because Y2K is in the same department as the honors and senior-year experience programs, it has been easy to collaborate with them as a source for upper-level mentors. Mentors can fulfill a course assignment for the senior-year seminar (KSU 4401) or satisfy a program requirement in applied learning for the honors program. The mentors also benefit from having to reflect on their undergraduate education and gaining experience as a mentor.

Challenges

The main challenge with this program has been recruiting sophomores to be protégés. (Moreover, several of the students who have participated in the program were, in fact, first-year students.) Recruitment has consisted of distributing flyers in the residential areas and the annual Majors Fair sponsored by KSU's advising and career services centers. We have also tried mass-mailing postcards to all students who have completed 24 to 48 credit hours. Despite these efforts, we have only been able to recruit a limited number of protégés. Also, several students who signed up to be protégés early in the semester were no longer responsive once mentor matches had been identified. Another challenge has been the commitment of protégés to meet with their mentors more than one or two times.

Despite the challenges, those protégés who remained involved with the program report that it has been beneficial to them and, in some cases, has helped them make a decision about a major. The key is convincing sophomores of the value of the program and encouraging them to commit for the entire semester. At present, there is no concrete incentive for participation for protégés (e.g., course credit), and the program relies on sophomores recognizing the value offered by working with a mentor.

UpperCLASS: Sophomore Learning Communities

Program Specifics

UpperCLASS translates the learning community structure and experience to the sophomore year and/or to courses that lead to a specific major. We have experimented with two sophomore-level learning communities so far: (a) criminal justice majors (spring 2005, spring 2006) and (b) teacher education majors (fall 2005, spring 2006, fall 2006). In fall 2006, we also piloted two sophomore learning communities for business majors, and we are currently planning one for students interested in the gender and women's studies minor.

UpperCLASS helps create cohorts for students entering into a major. Another primary objective is to enable faculty to address particular issues (e.g., diversity, off-campus experiences) across all courses in a way that both reinforces those issues and provides a multi-disciplinary perspective on them. Like KSU's first-year learning communities, UpperCLASS tries to capitalize on out-of-class engagement between faculty and students in order to develop deeper relationships than in stand-alone courses. Each learning community organizes some type of extracurricular activity to foster these connections and often these activities focus on career aspirations rather than issues concerning the first-year transition. In a sophomore learning community designed for business students, we planned out-of-class presentations by business leaders as well as the dean of the college of business.

The pilot Criminal Justice Learning Community included: (a) HS 2233 Overview of Human Services, (b) SPAN 2030 Spanish for Human Services and Criminal Justice Majors, and (c) CRJU 4430 Victimology. All three courses are requirements or upper-division electives for the major. The second iteration of the community consisted of only SPAN 2030 and CRJU 4430 to simplify registration procedures for students, especially since "a conflict-free registration process" has been identified as an issue "significantly more important to the public college sophomore" (Juillerat, 2000, p. 23).

The pilot Education Learning Community included (a) EDUC 2201 Teaching and Schools in a Changing Society, (b) *either* EDUC 2204 Human Growth, Development and Learning for Elementary Education majors *or* EDUC 2202 Life Span Development: Adolescent and Young Adulthood Emphasis for secondary education majors, and (c) ENGL 2110 World Literature. These courses are either lower-division major or general education requirements. Subsequent versions of the community consisted of only EDUC 2201 and ENGL 2110, again in order to simplify registration.

Learning outcomes for the UpperCLASS program are defined as follows:

- Students participating in Y2K Sophomore Learning Communities will connect with an academic program thoughtfully and purposefully to include: (a) connecting with a professional (i.e., professor, employer) in the field, (b) understanding the range of career possibilities associated with a given academic major, and (c) understanding the connection between undergraduate education and career.

- Students participating in Y2K Sophomore Learning Communities will connect socially with their peers to include engaging in at least one social activity outside the classroom with other students in the learning community during the semester.
- Students participating in Y2K Sophomore Learning Communities will connect what they are learning across the courses in the community to include completing at least one assignment that incorporates material from more than one class in the community.
- Students participating in Y2K Sophomore Learning Communities will understand the opportunities for experiential learning within the major sponsoring the community to include attending, either in or out of class, at least one presentation that discusses the opportunities for cooperative education, service-learning, and internships related to the major.

Challenges

By its very nature, learning communities require intensive and generous collaboration with other academic departments. We have been lucky at KSU to have had enthusiastic involvement from other departments. It is not always easy, because creating relationships with other departments depends on a combination of sympathetic personalities in these other departments and proactive outreach to them.

There has been positive instructor and student feedback on sophomore learning communities. Many students in the education community have been transfer students who appreciated the opportunity to get to know some of their fellow students. In fact, several of them developed friendships that extended beyond the classroom and coursework. One faculty member from the criminal justice community had this to say about her experience: "This class was one of the most positive and interactive classes that I have taught. I attribute it to the learning community. Specifically, the students seemed to have more common interests, to be more comfortable interacting, and had more opportunity to interact than in other classes I have taught. It may also be attributable to the small size of the class."

However, as with Major Mentors, we have had trouble encouraging student participation in UpperCLASS. Unlike with first-year learning communities and orientation, we do not have an opportunity to address most students directly about UpperCLASS and encourage their participation (let alone a requirement to enroll). Up to this point, recruitment has consisted of mass e-mailings to targeted student populations (e.g., based on major and credit-hour parameters), distribution of flyers in appropriate classes, and announcements at transfer-student orientations. Other factors might be student perceptions and uncertainty of the learning community structure; students either may feel that they do not require "special treatment" or may not even understand what a learning community is. It is important that sophomores are informed of the necessity and appropriateness of a learning community after the first year. Sophomores may find scheduling challenging and may need assistance from their advisors when registering.

Again, as with Major Mentors, when the communities have worked, they have worked well. Transfer students, in particular, could benefit greatly from these communities. The communities also have the potential to "support students in their ongoing search for healthy relationships [so that] we can encourage students to join new organizations, work in new small groups, or do whatever it takes to expand their friendships and to see relationships as choices" (Schaller, 2005, p. 23).

Conclusions and Recommendations

Thus far, implementation of sophomore programming has been relatively slow at KSU. In part, this has been a conscious decision to experiment with only a few initiatives at a time and on a manageable scale. Being a medium-sized public institution, it would be near impossible to institute an across-the-board initiative for all (or even the majority of) sophomores at KSU. As compared to campuses with traditional student populations and more clearly defined progression through class designations (i.e., first-year, sophomore, junior, senior), KSU's student population is harder to pin down in terms of identity as sophomores, as well as enrollment patterns (i.e., there are only a few general education courses that students would typically take in their sophomore year).

While some students have benefited from Y2K, there has also been a limited response from students to the offerings we have tested. Without a doubt, the main problem we have faced with our sophomore programs has been an inversion of the "if-you-build-it-they-will-come" phenomenon. The central problem is encouraging students to participate in programs that would likely help them succeed without imposing curricular or graduation requirements, offering course credit, or relying on significant amounts of funding.

The answer might very well be by persisting through the obstacles in order to generate word-of-mouth publicity about Y2K. Once we are able to recruit students more effectively, the sophomore learning communities and the Major Mentors program have definite promise for supporting sophomores in their transition into a major. They also require few additional resources because they build on existing courses and programs. Although we do not have enough data to establish effectiveness definitively, the preliminary evidence is promising for structures like peer mentoring and learning communities in helping sophomores connect with other students and with the institution.

Recommendations

It perhaps goes without saying that sophomore initiatives need to grow out of the unique identity of the campus and the culture that has evolved there. Nevertheless, for medium- to large-size, public institutions like KSU that serve a large percentage of transfer, nonresidential, and nontraditional students, there may be lessons that are transferable from programs at smaller and/or more traditional student populations.

With a program like Y2K that does not have a standing budget, collaboration is key. Effective collaboration will require a combination of proactive outreach to other departments and identification of sympathetic personalities who are open to initiatives that support student success. Further, initiatives that are premised on reciprocal benefits, as with our Major Mentors program, can obviate the need for financial resources.

Since sophomore programs cannot rely on structures that enable the success of first-year programs—for example, orientation—and sophomores are less of a "captive audience," the ability to contact students through e-mail or regular mail communication is crucial for advertising programs. However, this requires that the institution maintains up-to-date records of students' contact information and that students use these accounts. Public institutions need to recognize that their sophomore populations may differ from those at private institutions. As Juillerat (2000) makes clear, their needs and priorities do not necessarily align with their peers at private institutions. Yet, this does not mean that there are not lessons to be shared across institutional types.

Even at an institution like KSU, there is a significant population of traditional-age residential students who experience the same developmental issues as their peers at the traditional liberal arts college. And as KSU begins to serve more traditional-age residential students, sophomore initiatives based in residential life (e.g., living-learning communities, social activities targeting sophomores) may very well help in forging a more coherent sense of identity for KSU sophomores, which could help reinforce a sophomore identity on the rest of campus. Furthermore, some sophomore issues likely cut across institutional type. While the personal development issues for sophomores are crucial, we should not lose sight of the structural elements of the undergraduate experience that also contribute to the sophomore slump: connecting with a major and a department, navigating the general education curriculum in an intentional way, balancing working and studying (in practical ways but also at the level of values).

Our sophomore learning communities offer a promising support structure for transfer students who enter an institution with sophomore status. Not only does it enable social integration, it also streamlines the registration process, as it does with first-year students. When the mentor and protégé were able to truly connect, students reported that the Major Mentors program very much assisted in their perception of a major. We must now figure out how to connect and advertise these programs to our sophomores (which also presumes their identification as sophomores) and convince them that our programs are worth their time.

References

Anderson, E., & Schreiner, L. A. (2000). Advising for sophomore success. In L. A. Schreiner & J. Pattengale (Eds.), *Visible solutions for invisible students: Helping sophomores succeed* (Monograph No. 31, pp. 55-65). Columbia, SC: University of South Carolina, National Resource Center for The First-Year Experience and Students in Transition.

Board of Regents of the University System of Georgia. (2006). *Core mission statement for State universities in the University System of Georgia*. Retrieved September 27, 2006, from http://www.usg.edu/inst/mission/stateuniv.phtml.

Boivin, M., Fountain, G. A., & Baylis, B. (2000). Meeting the challenges of the sophomore year. In L. A. Schreiner & J. Pattengale (Eds.), *Visible solutions for invisible students: Helping sophomores succeed* (Monograph No. 31, pp. 1-18). Columbia, SC: University of South Carolina, National Resource Center for The First-Year Experience and Students in Transition.

Center for Institutional Effectiveness. (2004). A fresh look at traditional and nontraditional undergraduates at KSU. Kennesaw, GA: Kennesaw State University. Retrieved September 24, 2006, from http://ir.kennesaw.edu/documents/pdf/study/study_trad_nontrad_ug_200308.pdf.

Evenbeck, S. E., Boston, M., DuVivier, R. S., & Hallberg, K. (2000). Institutional approaches to helping sophomores. In L. A. Schreiner & J. Pattengale (Eds.), *Visible solutions for invisible students: Helping sophomores succeed* (Monograph No. 31, pp. 77-87). Columbia, SC: University of South Carolina, National Resource Center for The First-Year Experience and Students in Transition.

Flanagan, W. J. (1991). *Sophomore retention: The missing strategy in small college retention efforts* Unpublished doctoral dissertation, University of Wisconsin, Madison, 1991.

"Graduate with A's": Kennesaw State University's retention, progression & graduation improvement plan. (2005, November 14). Report submitted to the Board of Regents of the University System of Georgia.

Horn, L., & Malizio, A. (1998). *Undergraduates who work: National postsecondary student aid study,* 1996 (National Center for Education Statistics, U.S. Department of Education, Office of Educational Research and Improvement Publication No. NCES 98-137). Washington DC: U.S. Government Printing Office.

Juillerat, S. (2000). Assessing the expectations and satisfaction levels of sophomores: How are they unique? In L. A. Schreiner & J. Pattengale (Eds.), *Visible solutions for invisible students: Helping sophomores succeed* (Monograph No. 31, pp. 79-87). Columbia, SC: University of South Carolina, National Resource Center for The First-Year Experience and Students in Transition.

Kennesaw State University. (2006). Institutional Mission. Retrieved September 24, 2006, from http://www.kennesaw.edu/about/mission.shtml.

Pattengale, J., & Schreiner, L. A. (2000). What is the sophomore slump and why should we care? In L. A. Schreiner & J. Pattengale (Eds.), *Visible solutions for invisible students: Helping sophomores succeed* (Monograph No. 31, pp. v-viii). Columbia, SC: University of South Carolina, National Resource Center for The First-Year Experience and Students in Transition.

Schaller, M. (2005, July-August). Wandering and wondering: Traversing the uneven terrain of the second college year. *About Campus, 10*, 17-24.

Schreiner, L. A., & Pattengale, J. (Eds.). *Visible solutions for invisible students: Helping sophomores succeed* (Monograph No. 31). Columbia, SC: University of South Carolina, National Resource Center for The First-Year Experience and Students in Transition.

Chapter 7

The Sophomore-Year Experience (SYE) at Colgate University: A Case Study

Kimberly Taylor & Rajesh N. Bellani

At Colgate University, students in each year have a different focus: First-years are transitioning in, a majority of juniors study abroad, and seniors are job searching and preparing for graduate school. Yet, the sophomore year seems to be a "lost year" on our campus, as it is on many campuses. In fall 2002, the University launched a year-long planning effort to examine the history and key concepts of our student affairs program. The division felt we needed to be more intentional in our programming, especially with sophomore students. As a result of this examination, a comprehensive plan, the Vision for Residential Education, was launched. This plan sought to address various campus life issues specific to Colgate as well as those reflected in higher education in general.

One component of this was the Sophomore-Year Experience: The Arts of Democracy, which was launched in fall 2003 with support from the Carnegie Mellon Foundation. The SYE built on our successful First-Year Experience/Life Skills program but addressed issues more specific to sophomore concerns and their development. It focused more specifically on civil society and the skills necessary for an informed and engaged citizenry as a way to build and define the second year. In order to understand this initiative, it is important to also understand Colgate as an institution and the ideas that guided the implementation of this comprehensive program. Specifics regarding Colgate's SYE program will follow.

Institutional Context

Founded in 1819, Colgate University is a highly selective, residential liberal arts college located in central New York. Colgate's 2,700 students outnumber the 1,800 permanent residents of the small village of Hamilton. Colgate is unique among small liberal arts colleges in that it competes at the NCAA Division I level. Although a small university, the campus is a very busy one, with a common theme among students being "work hard, play hard."

Being a residential university allows us to create a semi-closed community where we can structure an educational process based on the very best thinking about personal development and educational theory. At the heart of this idea, is that we seek to educate the whole person:

> Colgate takes very seriously the idea that we produce students with the integrity, intellect, social imagination, humor, and passion that prepare them to recognize and realize their dreams, while serving as wise and ethical stewards of a free world and leaders of a democratic society. In doing so, we capture the essence of liberal arts education—the development of an engaged heart and a creative mind, which are connected to form a whole person. A liberal arts education is an education for the individual as well as the common good. (Weinberg, 2003, p. 324).

However, students do not always see this intimate setting in a positive way, referring to the "Colgate Bubble" as a way of describing the protective shield that can separate them from the real world. When we began to examine our campus culture, one of the things we sought to do was to expand this bubble a bit and, perhaps, even to pop it. We wanted to maintain many elements about Colgate, but we also felt we needed to better prepare our students for life beyond the college.

Several key events provided an impetus for us to examine our culture. For example, in November 2000, a drunk driving accident occurred on our campus that took the lives of four students, including a first-year Colgate student. This tragic event forced us to think about our culture, our college, and how our students lived their daily lives. We began to examine the drinking culture on campus and consider what kinds of social alternatives we were providing students in this small community. Colgate was, and is, far from unique regarding students' social choices. However, we were in a unique position, with a new president, a supportive dean of the college, and a mandate from our board to trustees to rethink our university, particularly in regard to student life. The previous year's tragedy also motivated us to take steps to enhance our students' residential lives in healthy ways.

Like many other first-year initiatives, Colgate's flourishing FYE program is structured to support a student's transition to higher education and independent living within a community. We focus on the basics of living with another person, managing time, joining organizations, while also dealing with the common first-year problems of homesickness and academic challenges. The SYE needed to take these individual skills and help students learn to build community, enhance their academic experiences, and begin to think about life beyond Colgate. We started out with a very theoretical framework of public work and community, and then narrowed our focus to specifics.

Thinking Broadly: The Theory Behind the Arts of Democracy

Public work is a conception of democracy and civic education championed by Jefferson, de Tocqueville, Dewey, Franklin, and others. It situates civic education as preparation for democratic living by having students work with other people to identify everyday problems, see opportunities, and become group problem solvers. The goal is to help students develop the skills, values, habits, and knowledge to do public work as part of the everyday. Underlying this goal is an unyielding belief that citizens can cocreate the decisions and actions needed to build and sustain healthy and vibrant communities. Thus, civic education is about teaching students to become cocreators of public goods with people they may not know, may not like, or from whom they may differ. The process of cocreation and its products (e.g., public goods and healthy communities) can anchor the lives of individuals. However, this is not easy work, nor is it a short-term goal.

Sophomores are the ideal population of students with whom to foster democratic principles because they have successfully transitioned from the first college year. During that first year, administrators act as authority figures, creating a safe community for students to acclimate to new surroundings and the rigors of academia. Sophomores begin the second year with established social groups and relationships, seeking opportunities to test their leadership skills and figure out their own place in the university.

At the same time, an emphasis on civic engagement helps foster student development in moral reasoning and of identity. An individual's personal identity and how he or she participates in a community are intertwined, especially because the college years are frequently spent engaging in the process of "meaning making" (Park, 2005). Students must determine who they are and how they fit into the world. Because development frequently occurs in response to perceived crisis, students need to have experiences that create an internal conflict allowing for reflection and growth (Evans, 1996). The sophomore year is a pivotal year in student development because students begin to encounter important internal and external life-course decisions. Moreover, it is a time of indecision where small efforts can dramatically shift the frameworks that sophomores have about themselves and their relationship to community (Weinberg, 2003).

As citizens of numerous communities, student examination of their place in society is critical to both the individual and to those with whom they interact in their private and public lives. Public work expands our definition of democracy beyond formal political structures to resituate it back within communities. This is a vision of democracy that accepts the messy and complex state of the human condition, while embracing the belief that people can work with others to create goods that improve lives and build healthy communities. Colby, Ehrlich, Beaumont, and Stephens (2003) make a compelling case that civic education must include:

- *Community connections.* Students need to have a diverse set of experiences within different types of communities. These experiences are essential for helping students develop the sense of what it means to belong to a community and why modern citizenship entails being members of multiple communities.
- *Moral and civic value.* We need a clear and consistent set of central values and virtues of democracy and citizenship built into our programs. These values and virtues have to be presented and reinforced to take hold.
- *Systematic social responsibility.* Very few students bring life experiences of active civic engagement. We need programs that provide students opportunities to explore public issues, to understand democratic process, and to develop an interest in public policy, social justice, or the common good in its broadest sense. Students need to develop systematic understandings and ways to care about and act on frameworks of social responsibility that guide their everyday actions.

However, the implementation of such lofty ideas are not without challenges. For example, we recognized the need to differentiate between being an engaged campus and a campus that was promoting civic education. Further, we recognized that a focus on values alone was inadequate; we also needed to focus on skills and habits. Finally, we had to bridge the division between academic and student affairs if our efforts were to be successful. With these challenges in mind, we developed three guiding questions to help us in the planning process:

1. What are the skills, habits, values, and knowledge that our students will need to be prepared for the 21st century?
2. What do students do or want to do outside the classroom?
3. How can we ensure that students are acquiring these skills, habits, values, and knowledge as they are doing the things they want to do?

Development of the Sophomore-Year Experience

We were extremely fortunate to have support and direction from the office of our president as well as generous financial support from the Carnegie Mellon Foundation. With this institutional support, we formulated specific ideas and began to develop a comprehensive program. Our research indicated that the Arts of Democracy program needed to do the following:

- Develop the skills for citizenship including public speaking, active listening, problem solving, and the ability to "walk across difference"
- Enhance students' academic experience by capturing the educational moments outside the classroom
- Create a sense of community and engage peers in discussions about humanity and oppression

- Build bridges between community service and collaborative experience and encourage student reflection on these themes
- Develop leadership and skill-training enterprises
- Advance active engagement in activities as a central component of the learning process
- Engage people with differing points of view (Loeb, 1999)
- Use relationships and foster involvement with faculty and alumni
- Promote collaboration with student affairs departments (e.g. Career Services; Women's Studies; LGBTQ; Residential Life; ALANA—African, Latin American, Asian American, and Native American Cultures; Religious Life)
- Use peer-to-peer education
- Develop participatory governance where students can initiate and witness change similar to town hall meetings (Rimmerman, 2001)

A great deal of time was spent defining the Arts of Democracy succinctly and in ways that 18- to 22-year-olds could identify with and value. In order to develop this language, we spent a lot of time with the experts—the students themselves. After conducting many focus groups in spring 2003, we learned that students wanted a program that contained the following elements:

- Student choice and voice
- Interactive, engaging, and organic programs
- Safe environments where different points of view can be expressed
- Faculty involvement outside the classroom
- Social events that involve class community

Following the focus groups, we designed several simple goals to guide the launch of SYE in fall 2003:

- Publicize the existence of the SYE to the Class of 2006
- Develop a strong sophomore class council program
- Develop a program building upon and expanding current programs offered by student and academic affairs

Sophomore-Year Experience Programs

Sophomore Class Council Events

Communication about the SYE program was a concern and challenge. College students are deluged with e-mails, and Colgate students have developed a strategy for dealing with this: They delete most of what comes from the university. This problem was greatly ameliorated through the development and cultivation of the sophomore class council. Differing from the Student Government Association (SGA), the nine-member class council has a representative in SGA but takes on the additional task of creating programs within the sophomore class that help develop class unity. The class council model was vital for our success with first-year initiatives as council members effectively and enthusiastically communicated with the class about events and programs. This peer-to-peer education also demonstrated the public work model we hoped to promote. We work with the Sophomore Class Council to think about how they can facilitate efforts by all sophomores to build community and create things of lasting value for the campus.

Rather than create programs for students, we wanted the class council to get sophomores to work with each other to create projects. In 2003, they started a Student Lecture Forum to present research done in classes about public issues to each other, revived the debate team, helped develop new policies and procedures for campus, and developed a sophomore-to-sophomore mentorship program in the community. The council has also sponsored social events such as foam dance parties, all-sophomore barbeques, a “bring back the date” speed-dating event, study abroad information sessions, and welcome back dinners. Beyond these programming efforts, the class council also allows us to get valuable ideas and feedback from students.

Now beginning our fourth year, we have developed a comprehensive program that is interwoven into the fabric of the university. When we devised this program, we sought to include as many of our university resources as possible. This collaborative approach institutionalizes the initiative and provides students with a program that is visible in many parts of their college experience. In particular, we think about our program as having four components: (a) academic/faculty, (b) alumni programs, (c) career development, and (d) social. As one will see, many of these programs fall into more than one category. This was an intentional aspect of our work toward creating a seamless program. Not all of our programs were a resounding success. Looking back on our work, the most successful initiatives were those that were created with the intentional goal of developing skills in an engaging way. The following are programs we have developed and improved upon over the past three years.

Democracy Dinners

This weekly dinner series provides groups of 15 sophomores with opportunities to have conversations with faculty and alumni regarding a specific area of expertise. Held at our faculty club/restaurant, we invite students by sending out an e-mail message about the featured guest and accept students on a first-come, first-served basis. We use a variety of techniques to engage a range of the sophomores in the program by including faculty from various departments. Discussion topics have included social and cultural trends in society, issues of global and community oppression, campus diversity, and study abroad experiences. In our first year, 370 students (nearly 50% of the class) participated in the dinners.

Dialogue Circles

Faculty and staff are trained for eight weeks in the fall semester before moderating six week-long conversations about democracy, diversity, and pluralism. These sustained dialogues are specifically designed to increase intellectual diversity on campus by encouraging conversation around race, gender, sexual orientation, and socioeconomics.

Dinner and a Good Book

Advancing conversation and building relationships, this SYE program brings together students, faculty, and staff members. We launched this program in the summer of 2005 after having conversations with students about how they missed reading for fun. We sent out an e-mail message in June to 750 rising sophomores, with a list of six books. Students were able to choose as many books as they liked and read them over the summer. After they attend a dinner with a chosen faculty member to discuss the book, students are reimbursed for half the book’s purchase price. In fall of 2005, 104 students chose to participate in this program; however, a concern was that the vast majority (95) of them were women. To encourage greater participation from male students, we are reexamining the kinds of texts we select. Students have also begun to request particular texts and are inviting faculty with differing opinions to moderate discussions that promote more than one point of view.

Living-Learning Community

Twenty-five sophomores are currently living together and taking a course on the psychology of leadership that is taught in the residence hall. Taught by a senior member of the psychology department, the course includes alumni guest speakers and culminates in self-designed, independent student projects. Selected classes are run by students, who gather common readings, moderate the discussion, and interview alumni participants. As a class, this group has visited the Bronx Zoo to view primate leadership qualities, the United States Holocaust Memorial Museum to discuss Hitler's style of leadership, and the National Mall to explore public remembrance of U.S. social and political leaders.

United States Holocaust Memorial Museum Trip

An annual endowed SYE trip to Washington, DC, focuses on ideas of social oppression and activism. Approximately 50 students spend two days in Washington, DC, visiting the Holocaust Museum, meeting with a survivor, and participating in academic activities. In October 2006, students from the Department of Peace and Conflict Studies visited the United Institute for Peace, Amnesty International, and Committee for Conscience of the Holocaust Museum. Students attended presentations focused on the crisis in Darfur and the response of humanitarian organizations. Back on campus, interested students met with the Colgate chapter of Amnesty International to discuss how to involve other members of the Colgate community in matters of social justice.

Non-Governmental Organizations (NGO) Alternative Spring Break

This week-long trip to Washington, DC, provides an opportunity for 12 sophomores, chosen through an extensive application process, to explore NGOs and attend graduate-level philanthropy seminars at Georgetown University. To prepare for this trip, students are provided with readings and attend dinners with Colgate faculty who discuss leadership styles as well their own experiences with NGOs. While in Washington, students visit various nonprofit organizations that have been chosen in response to their specific interests. Students also spend time with alumni in the area, discussing public work and career and internship opportunities. When they return to Colgate, students meet with alumni to discuss their work in Washington and have an opportunity to attend grant writing classes. They are also expected to keep journals and provide substantive evaluations of their experience.

Student Philanthropy Council

This fund provides an opportunity for 10 sophomores, supervised by a faculty member, to distribute money to nonprofit organizations in the Central New York area. Students learn how to assess the fiscal responsibility and operations of an organization. This also provides students with an additional connection to the community, encouraging them to see themselves as a part of the civic process.

Sophomore-to-Sophomore Program

A small group of sophomores developed a mentoring program with the local public high school. Colgate sophomores hosted the local community's high school sophomore class for a day at the university, fostering a closer relationship with the high school students and making them more comfortable on campus. Colgate students had lunch with the students, talked with them about college admissions, and invited a popular faculty member to provide a keynote. More than

60 Colgate sophomores volunteered their time for this day and met one-on-one with high school sophomores.

Résumé Challenge

While résumé writing is sometimes a task reserved for juniors and seniors, our students are increasingly searching for summer internships and fellowships during their sophomore year. Additionally, all of our student leadership positions require résumés from applicants. Even if a sophomore is not considering these options, we believe that the act of creating a résumé encourages a student to look at the choices they have made and where their passions and interests lie. Recognizing the competitive nature of our students, the Résumé Challenge encourages residential advisors to devise creative ways to collect the most résumés on their floor. The RA who receives the most résumés receives a prize. The sophomore students who have completed a peer-reviewed résumé receive personal business cards and the opportunity to attend an alumni networking reception. Our first year, more than 40% of our sophomore class had a résumé on file in career services. This was a substantial increase from previous years.

Challenges

As one can see, particularly from a theoretical perspective, we established some lofty goals. One of our biggest challenges in the implementation and continuation of the SYE program has been figuring out how to encourage students to voluntarily create programs that are meaningful to them. None of our programs are mandatory for students. This would, in many ways, defy the purpose of encouraging students to examine what is important to them. However, by doing this, we miss a large portion of the student body who may need to be engaged the most. Although participation in some of our programs, such as the "dinner and a good book," exceeded our expectations, we are still working on how to encourage less-engaged students to take advantage of other programs such as the trips to Washington, DC, and democracy dinners.

Gender has also been an issue. Women are definitely over-represented in our programs. We have been doing research in this area and have found at least three problems in our approaches. First, college men may be intimidated by the idea of intimate discussion over dinner. They are concerned about not being able to respond effectively and do not feel comfortable in a formal setting. Also, college men are much more likely to go to an event in a group, and most of our events focus on individual rather than group participation. Additionally, we have not included many active events (e.g., games, rock-climbing) to build community. Such as activities may be more appealing to male students. We are beginning to address these issues.

We are also still working on engaging diverse members of our campus. We are a predominantly White campus and although diversity has definitely increased in the past five years, sharp divisions still exist, and underrepresented students are concerned that their needs are not being met. The self-reported experiences of students of color and their level of satisfaction on our campus differ greatly from majority students. If we are to live up to our ideal of teaching students to "walk across difference," the SYE must do a better job of engaging students in discussions about these issues.

We also have not been able to get a clear assessment of how our programs are affecting students. We have some terrific anecdotal data based on qualitative evaluations, but these are largely from students who participate vigorously in many of our programs. It is difficult to determine whether the sophomore-year experience programs have had an effect on the larger campus culture.

Despite these challenges, our work on the sophomore year has had a transformative effect on our division and on the University as a whole. Initially, it informed the university-wide strategic plan announced in October 2003, particularly in regard to three important goals that shaped the development of the SYE:

- Reinterpreting the liberal arts skills of communication and critical thinking to take into account 21st-century challenges and opportunities
- Multiplying connections between students and faculty members by building on the faculty's record of original research and creativity
- Building on Colgate's strong sense of community, locally and globally

Moreover, our entire division was transformed as a result of a focus on citizenship and engagement. Like so many other colleges and universities, we moved away from a consumer-driven, customer service model to one based on teaching skills of leadership and ownership. We replaced the Office of Student Activities with the Center for Leadership and Student Involvement (CLSI). We stopped hiring programmers who would plan things for students to do. Instead, we hired mentors who could work with students to transform campus organizations into civic educational experiences.

We have made great strides and developed a comprehensive sophomore program, but we still have a lot of work to do. Our great advantage, of course, like any other institution of higher education, is that every year we have a brand new group of sophomore students who are eager to try new things and think about their lives in fresh and exciting ways. Although the challenges are great, we are very fortunate to be able to work with such a population.

References

Colby, A., Ehrlich T., Beaumont E., & Stephens, J. (2003). *Educating citizens: Preparing America's undergraduates for lives of moral responsibility and civic responsibility*. San Francisco: The Carnegie Foundation For The Advancement of Teaching.

Evans, N. J. (1996). Theories of student development. In S. R. Komives & D. B. Woodward, Jr. (Eds.), *Student Services: A handbook for the profession* (pp. 164-187). New York: Holt, Rinehart, and Winston.

Loeb, P. R. (1999). *Soul of a citizen: Living with conviction in a cynical time*. New York, NY: St. Martin Griffen.

Park, C. L. (2005). Religion as a meaning-making framework in coping with life stress. *Journal of Social Issues, 61*(4), 707-729.

Rimmerman, C. (2001). *The new citizenship*. Boulder, CO: Westview Press.

Weinberg, A. (2003, Summer). The road to education for democracy. *Academic Exchange Quarterly*, 331-335.

Chapter 8

Learning from the Best: Recommendations for Sophomore Initiatives

Barbara F. Tobolowsky & Bradley E. Cox

This monograph captures many of the most recent initiatives intentionally designed for second-year college students. While a few campuses have comprehensive and proven programs (e.g., Beloit College), most institutions have only recently turned their attention to the specific needs of their second-year students. Findings from the National Survey of Sophomore Initiatives (see chapter 2) suggest that most sophomore programs are relatively new or still in the planning stages. Yet, this chapter is able to offer a range of recommendations based on the previous chapters and the submissions to the unpublished *Exploring the Evidence* monograph on sophomore programs. These recommendations are relevant for both those campuses that are beginning to consider sophomore initiatives and those campuses that are looking to improve or expand already established offerings for second-year students.

Getting it Right from the Start

Planning and implementing sophomore-specific initiatives, while potentially challenging, need not be an overwhelming task. The following three recommendations offer strategies for making the process administratively efficient and educationally effective.

- *Learn from the students themselves.* Sophomore initiatives can only be effective if they address the specific needs and challenges of second-year students. While this monograph and other national research provide a general overview, the experiences of second-year students are unique to individual institutions. Campuses should begin by gathering data that help illuminate the experiences of second-year students at that institution. The institutional research office can provide information about sophomore student enrollment, retention, grades, courses, activities, and other data of interest. Focus groups or interviews provide important access to the student voice—and to experiences that cannot be gleaned from a spreadsheet. Administering a survey instrument that asks students about their experiences as sophomores is a useful strategy that permits data collection from a much larger group of students. With these data in hand, institutions can target sophomore initiatives toward the specific challenges faced by their institution's second-year students.
- *Perform a campus audit.* Before developing new initiatives for sophomores, campuses should examine the programs and services that are already in place. Such an audit may reveal the existence of a number of sophomore-specific programs. If those programs are independent, they can be repackaged under the umbrella of a comprehensive sophomore program (see for

example, Colorado College in chapter 5). In addition, it may be pertinent to consider the various non-sophomore-specific policies and programs that nonetheless affect sophomores. For example, how do current housing allocation or course registration procedures affect sophomores? The audit process should also examine any initiatives already in place for first-year students on the campus. Following the model established at Beloit College, institutions may be able to build on these programs and expand them into the second year.

- *Don't work alone.* Efforts to improve the sophomore-year experience will likely need to include both academic and social components. Therefore, the most effective initiatives will emerge through a partnership between academic and student affairs. It is only through the cooperation of the entire campus community that disparate initiatives can be integrated to create an intentional, comprehensive second-year experience.

Fostering Community for Second-Year Students

It is important that college students feel a part of the institutional community. For a first-year student, this sense of community is created by participation in orientation programs, residence halls, and common core classes. But these connections often disappear during the sophomore year. Therefore, many sophomores struggle to maintain a sense of community within the institution. However, implementation of sophomore-specific initiatives may help strengthen students' sense of community as second-year students. Examples of promising initiatives include:

- *Second-year seminars.* Seminars for first-year students are now nearly ubiquitous on college campuses. Far fewer institutions, however, offer seminars specifically for second-year students. But those institutions that did offer such courses found positive outcomes similar to those typically found in first-year seminars—chief among them, connections to peers and the institution. Seminars may also provide an avenue through which an institution can convey important information to sophomore students. For example, SUNY-Binghampton has a two-credit career development course specifically for sophomores. DePaul University requires all second-year students to take a seminar, which is a core curriculum requirement, about multiculturalism.
- *Living-learning communities.* Living-learning communities (LLCs) may hold considerable potential as sophomore-specific initiatives. As the name implies, LLCs integrate the social and academic aspects of the college experience. Now commonly offered for first-year students, these curricular efforts with a residential component have proven to be excellent ways to facilitate community and encourage student success. A few campuses (e.g., Texas Tech University, Kennesaw University) have adapted the concept for their second-year students and found similar benefits.
- *Class officers.* The establishment of sophomore class councils/officers may prove to be a cost-effective way to facilitate community among second-year students. Several institutions mentioned that they have sophomore councils or class officers (e.g., Wofford College) who speak on behalf of sophomores and plan events specifically for second-year students.
- *Retreats.* Though likely a financially expensive initiative, a sophomore class retreat can help sophomores reconnect with each other and the institution. Perhaps the oldest of these initiatives occurs at Beloit College; it has been conducting a sophomore retreat for 15 years. Assessment confirms the benefits accrued by students and the institution.
- *Traditions.* Each of the aforementioned initiatives offers opportunities to develop sophomore-specific traditions. These traditions can serve as a symbolic "rite of passage" that confirms students' shared transition into their second college year. For example, Emmanuel College

holds a Sophomore Pinning Ceremony where department chairs present each student in their major a pin bearing the college seal. Families are invited to attend the ceremony. Similarly, Duke University offers a "Bricks to Stone" pinning ceremony at the end of the first year as a way to mark the passage from first- to second-year status. Although Duke's program began as a residence life initiative, a diverse collection of campus offices are involved in the ceremony (e.g., advisors, librarians, the Office of the Provost, the Office of the President, the dean of students). For other campuses, the traditions may revolve around welcome back dances (e.g., Charleston Southern University), brunches (e.g., Daemen College), dinners (e.g., Colgate University, Loyola College, Yale University), or trips (e.g., Messiah College, Washington and Lee University).

Targeting Sophomores for Educationally Purposeful Activities

The sophomore year may be the ideal time for students to participate in a number of important educational activities. Though these activities need not be limited to sophomores, they may be particularly appropriate for second-year students. Therefore, you may wish to examine ways in which your institution can specifically target sophomores when encouraging participation in the following educational activities:

- *Undergraduate research.* Decades of studies have confirmed that student connections with faculty are critical to student success. Working with faculty on research helps forge those connections and helps challenge the student academically. This type of academic challenge is well timed with sophomores who, having succeeded in their first-year general education courses, may be ready to begin in-depth explorations of a particular discipline. Such exploration may also be appropriate as students make decisions regarding their majors—a choice often made after the sophomore year. Several schools offer undergraduates the opportunity to work with faculty on research, but Union College has an independent research program in which second-year students are targeted to work directly with a professor on his/her research. At the time of the National Survey of Sophomore-Year Initiatives, the program was only for honors students. However, Union's success with this program suggests second-year students, in general, would benefit from this opportunity as well.
- *Advising.* Good advising is the key to student success. For many students, advising is ad hoc until they declare a major. However, as students near making that decision, good advising is crucial. Where are their interests and skills? What majors and careers linked to those fields make sense for each student? At Emmanuel College, academic advisors for undeclared sophomores explore particular introductory courses that might assist students in narrowing their interests. Some institutions assign students an advisor when they come in, and they keep those advisors through the second year or until they declare a major (e.g., Barnard College). What is apparent, students need to know who to go to with questions, so the appointment must be clear to students from matriculation.
- *Career planning and major exploration.* At many institutions, students must declare a major during or immediately after their second year. During this stressful time, students may benefit from initiatives designed to help them explore potential majors and careers. Several of the schools responding to the survey offer major or career fairs in which students can speak with representatives of many programs/disciplines in one place. Creighton University, for example, presents a major fair jointly facilitated by the Career Center and the Center for Academic Planning. At Oregon State University, the Career Center partners with Housing

to offer sophomore housing communities that run activities designed to help students select a major and develop marketable job skills.

- *Leadership development.* Many sophomores are rewarded because of their leadership activities in the first year. For example, SUNY Fredonia offers leadership classes that are "geared toward second-year students" who were nominated at the end of their first year. Lehigh University gives the Blake Award to a sophomore student who "showed the best combination of academic achievement and leadership potential in their first year." Alternately, leadership development initiatives may target students who have been previously disengaged from the institution. At the University of Georgia, a program called *Navigation: Leadership* targets second-year students who have not yet become involved at the school.
- *Study abroad programs.* College students have, in recent years, increasingly spent part of their time in college studying overseas. Sophomores participating in these experiences may derive a number of benefits that will serve them well during the remainder of their college years. The institution may also benefit from the increased persistence of students who study abroad. One particularly successful program is offered at the University of Dallas. Their Rome Program was founded in 1970, and students become eligible to participate during their sophomore year. Institutional assessments have found that participating students were more likely to graduate in four years than similarly qualified students who did not go abroad (79% vs. 51% graduated within four years).
- *Student mentors.* Sophomores can take part in mentoring programs in two ways. First, institutions have professionals or advanced students serve as mentors for sophomore students. Such programs may help sophomores explore challenging issues and identify habits employed by successful students. SUNY-Binghamton's *Discovery Program*, for example, employs 25 peer advisors and 55 tutors who assist sophomores with degree planning and career exploration. Second, sophomore students can serve as mentors to first-year students. In these programs, sophomores can reinforce positive habits as they pass their wisdom on to new students. At Johns Hopkins University, for example, sophomores serve as peer mentors to students in first-year seminar courses. On other campuses, sophomores may work as resident advisors (e.g., Oglethorpe University) or in other leadership positions (e.g., Asbury College uses sophomores in their orientation program).

Communicating to Students is Key

Regardless of the extent or type of sophomore initiatives, communication is critical to the success of second-year students and institutional efforts to support them. Effective communication is also comparatively easy. But it is also frequently overlooked. Communication among staff/departments facilitates integration, collaboration, and the development of a comprehensive set of sophomore initiatives. Communication with students can help foster a sense of community and belonging among sophomores. And of course, various forms of communication can be used to encourage student participation in sophomore-specific initiatives.

Creating brochures, newsletters, or e-mails for sophomore students appears to be a relatively low-cost, less demanding way to start connecting with students. These publications are a great way to get information out to students—from relevant events to important deadlines. For instance, San Francisco State University sends e-mails to all rising sophomores outlining the process of course registration. At Oglethorpe University, sophomore class representatives send out e-mail newsletters to keep the class informed of relevant activities.

Some institutions use publications to convey topics besides basic information. Barnard College has produced a sophomore-specific publication highlighting the sophomore year as a rite of passage.

Some innovative institutions are using communication tools to combat the sophomore slump before students finish their first year on campus. One institution has even enlisted the help of parents. Lewis and Clark University sends letters to the parents of first-year students at the end of the year to discuss the idea of the "sophomore slump" and other sophomore issues.

Bringing it All Together

Though an institution may administer any number of these initiatives in relative isolation, the students experience these initiatives as a whole. Therefore, it is imperative that institutions consider all aspects of the sophomore year. Ideally, sophomore initiatives on a campus will be cumulative, connected, and complementary components of an intentionally comprehensive sophomore-year experience designed to foster student success.

This chapter provides a few of the many ideas that surfaced in the monograph, the National Survey of Sophomore-Year Initiatives, and the *Exploring the Evidence* submissions on sophomore programs. Hopefully, these ideas will help institutions begin to focus their attention on second-year students as they plan new programs or add to those already on campus. More important, we hope these ideas shed light on the experiences of these most-deserving students so that they can move from the shadows and enjoy increasing levels of learning and success.

About the Contributors

Rajesh N. Bellani is the special assistant to the vice president/dean of the college and associate dean of academic programs at Colgate University. As such, Bellani forges connections between academic and student affairs units, develops a scholars' program focused on leadership studies, and works with faculty to develop sophomore living-learning units. Formerly, as dean of the Sophomore-Year Experience, he was architect of Colgate's comprehensive, residential, sophomore-year initiative. Previous positions include assistant dean of multicultural affairs and director of the ALANA Cultural Center at Colgate University; inaugural director of student activities and leadership at Wesleyan University; director of new student orientation at the State University of New York at Geneseo; and assistant director of the Office of Student Programming at the College of the Holy Cross. Bellani has a doctorate in higher education from the University of Pennsylvania where he did research on sophomore men and their search for personal purpose. He also holds a master's degree in college student personnel from Western Illinois University and a bachelor's degree in political science from the State University of New York at Geneseo. He is a frequent presenter at student affairs conferences and university campuses on residential education programs and the sophomore-year experience.

Mimi Benjamin is the assistant to the vice president for student affairs and an adjunct faculty member in the Educational Leadership and Policy Studies program at Iowa State University. She received her Ph.D. in educational leadership and policy studies from Iowa State University, her M.A. in English from Clarion University of Pennsylvania, her M.Ed. in educational leadership from Ohio University, and her B.S. degree in secondary education/English from Clarion University of Pennsylvania. Benjamin was a coordinator of residence life at Iowa State University, the assistant director of residential life at Plymouth State College (now University), and a hall director at Plymouth State College before joining the vice president's office staff. A member of ACPA, ASHE and NASPA, Benjamin currently serves on the editorial board for the "Research in Brief" and "On the Campus" sections of the *Journal of College Student Development*. She was awarded the NASPA Region IV-East Mid-Level Professional award in 2005 and the national Mid-Level Professional Award from NASPA in 2006. Her research interests include learning communities, student affairs administration, undergraduate student experiences, and ethics.

Edward K. Chan directs the Year 2 Kennesaw program at Kennesaw State University in Georgia, where he is also an assistant professor of English and co-director of the Interdisciplinary Studies Degree Program. He received a Ph.D. in English from the University of Rochester in New York, an M.A. in English from California State University, Fullerton, and a B.A. in English from the University of California at Riverside. Chan has been working on sophomore issues at Kennesaw and with colleagues across the country since 2003. He was a panelist on the national teleconference

The Forgotten Student: Understanding and Supporting Sophomores (National Resource Center for The First-Year Experience and Students in Transition, 9 March 2006) and the national audio conference *Strategies for Sophomore Year Success* (PaperClip Communications, 7 December 2006). He has also worked as a research fellow for the Center of Inquiry in the Liberal Arts at Wabash College studying out-of-class engagement and with the National Survey of Student Engagement Institute on the Documenting Effective Educational Practices project.

Bradley E. Cox is a Ph.D. student in the Higher Education program at The Pennsylvania State University. Currently working on the *Parsing the First Year of College* project, Cox is a research assistant for Dr. Patrick Terenzini. Before joining the PSU program, Cox served as the coordinator of research and public information at the National Resource Center for The First-Year Experience and Students in Transition at the University of South Carolina. His research interests focus on two related areas: (a) the contextual factors that affect student aspirations for, access to, and success in higher education and (b) the vertical integration of educational systems.

William J. Flanagan is vice president for student affairs and dean of students at Beloit College in Wisconsin. Flanagan received his B.A. in American studies from St. Michael's College in Vermont, M.Ed. in student personnel administration from the University of Vermont, and his Ph.D. in educational administration from the University of Wisconsin-Madison. Flanagan has more than 30 years of experience in small college student affairs administration. Specific areas of expertise include first- and second-year programs designed to help students make the transition from high school to college and student affairs administration at small colleges. Flanagan has authored articles on both topics, consulted widely on the development of first- and second-year programs and retention, and is a consultant-evaluator for the North Central Association's Higher Learning Commission.

Ann M. Gansemer-Topf is the associate director of research for enrollment services at Iowa State University and formerly the associate director of institutional research at Grinnell College in Grinnell, Iowa. Prior to her work in institutional research, she was an academic advisor and taught and coordinated learning communities in the College of Design at Iowa State University. She has also worked in residence life and campus ministry. She received her Ph.D. in educational leadership and policy studies from Iowa State University, her M.S. in higher education from Iowa State University, and her B.A. in psychology from Loras College in Dubuque, Iowa. She was the recipient of the Research Excellence award from Iowa State University and was recognized as an Outstanding Academic Advisor from the College of Design at Iowa State University. She has presented at several national conferences, and her areas of interest include assessment of student learning, effective teaching/learning pedagogies, student persistence, and understanding campus cultures.

Jerry Pattengale speaks nationally and contributes regularly to the scholarship on student success, with an emphasis on purpose-guided approaches. He has published book chapters on student success in *Visible Solutions for Invisible Students* (National Resource Center for The First-Year Experience and Students in Transition, 2000) and *The Motivated Student* (McGraw-Hill, in press). Pattengale served on the advisory board for the National Resource Center for The First-Year Experience and Students in Transition and received the Outstanding First-Year Student Advocate award. Pattengale also received two Professor of the Year awards from students at Azusa Pacific University. He received his Ph.D. in ancient history and his M.A in Tutor Stuart history from Miami University, Ohio and his M.A. in interpersonal development from Wheaton College, Illinois. He currently serves as the assistant vice president for scholarship and grants at Indiana Wesleyan University.

Molly A. Schaller is an associate professor and coordinator of the College Student Personnel and Higher Education Administration programs and a fellow in the Learning Teaching Center at the University of Dayton. Prior to her faculty position, she worked for 10 years in student affairs administration. She holds a bachelor's degree in psychology from The Ohio State University, master's degree in college student personnel from Miami University, and a Ph.D. in higher education administration from Ohio University. Her research interests include college student development with specific focus on the sophomore student, student affairs in Catholic higher education, and the relationship between the physical environment and learning.

Laurie Schreiner is professor and director of the doctoral programs in higher education at Azusa Pacific University in southern California. Co-author of the *Student Satisfaction Inventory*, she spent 25 years in higher education as a psychology professor and associate academic dean prior to coming to Azusa Pacific. Her experience includes directing academic advising programs and first-year seminars, chairing retention and curriculum committees, and directing federally funded grant projects for first-year seminars and strengths-based approaches to student success and retention. Schreiner is co-author of the latest revision of *StrengthsQuest: Discover and Develop Your Strengths in Academics, Career, and Beyond* published by The Gallup Organization. She is co-editor of the monograph *Visible Solutions for Invisible Students: Helping Sophomores Succeed* and serves on the advisory board of the National Resource Center for The First-Year Experience and Students in Transition. She has consulted with more than 100 colleges and universities on issues of retention, academic advising, student satisfaction, and effective teaching strategies.

Stephanie K. Serven is the coordinator of commuter services, family programs, and leadership development at Marymount University in Arlington, Virginia. Previously, she worked at the National Resource Center for The First-Year Experience and Students in Transition as the graduate assistant for research and public information, assisting with research projects and the compilation and distribution of web-based resources. She earned her bachelor's degree in psychology from the College of the Holy Cross in Worcester, Massachusetts and her master's degree in higher education and student affairs from the University of South Carolina.

Joyce M. Stern is dean for student academic support and advising at Grinnell College. Her work over the last six years includes directing the College's advising program, co-directing the first-year seminar program, coordinating services for students with disabilities, serving on the academic standing committee, and identifying and reaching out to students experiencing academic difficulty. Stern is an alumna of Grinnell College, and she completed an M.A. in higher education administration from Stanford University. Her work experience is primarily in residence life and career development at several institutions including Lawrence University (residence director), California Polytechnic State University – San Luis Obispo (coordinator of student development), Scripps College (career counselor), and Coe College (director of career services). In her career, she has focused on the specific needs of first-year students, women, science students, students with mental health issues, and GLBT students.

Julie Tetley Stockenberg is the director of first-year and sophomore studies and advising at The Colorado College. In her role, she has developed a program specifically for second-year students titled the Sophomore Jump. She has several years of experience in teaching and advising and has given numerous presentations at the local, state, and national level. In addition, she serves as the chair for NACADA's Small Colleges and Universities Commission. She is currently enrolled in a doctoral program in the School of Education and Human Development at The George Washington University and the focus of her dissertation is on second-year students and institutional environments that promote self-authorship.

Kimberly Taylor is dean of the Sophomore-Year Experience (SYE) and administrative advisor at Colgate University. Following her experience as an educator in the history and sociology departments in the public schools, Taylor came to Colgate in 2003 as the coordinator of Democracy Projects to develop and implement the sophomore-year experience with Rajesh Bellani. As dean of the SYE, Taylor works closely with various academic and student affairs departments to develop and enhance programs that help teach the skills of active citizenship and personal reflection. Taylor is completing her master's thesis at Colgate University, a discussion of the role of democracy in higher education as it relates to socioeconomic class. She holds a bachelor's degree in history and pre-law studies from Syracuse University.

Barbara F. Tobolowsky is associate director of the National Resource Center for The First-Year Experience and Students in Transition. In this position, she has overall responsibility for the Center's research, conferences, and publication efforts. Tobolowsky also has a clinical faculty appointment in the Educational Leadership and Policies department at the University of South Carolina where she teaches several graduate seminars in the Higher Education Student Affairs (HESA) program. She earned her doctorate from the University of California, Los Angeles in higher education and organizational change.